Listen at 101 Greene Street.
New York, NY

SONOS
The Home Sound System

sonos.com/nyc

KVADRAT / RAF SIMONS

Paustian Furniture Collection
Paustian Modular Sofa
Design Erik Rasmussen

paustian

paustian.com

Reform

Reform offers architect-
designed kitchen fronts and
table tops that can easily be
combined with the popular
elements from IKEA®

www.reformcph.com

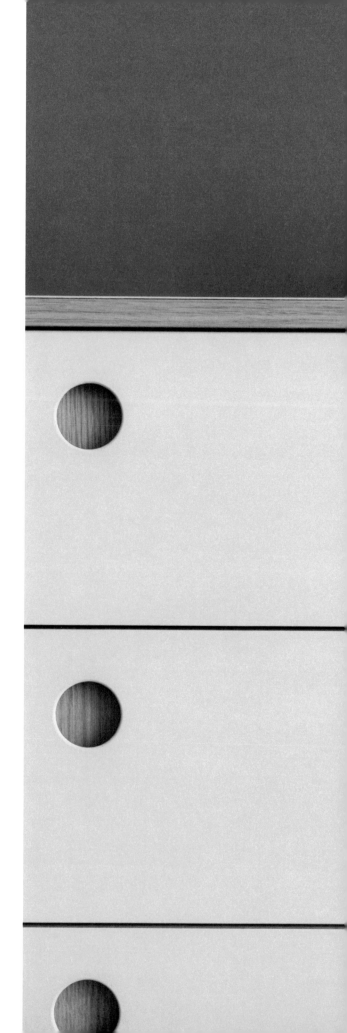

Basis 01 Linoleum / Soft mushroom / Eg

KINFOLK

Published by Ouur Media
Amagertorv 14, Level 1
1160 Copenhagen, Denmark
Telephone: +45 33 30 03 33

5210 N Williams Avenue
Portland, Oregon 97217 USA
Telephone: +1 503-946-8400

Kinfolk is a slow lifestyle magazine published
by Ouur Media that explores ways for readers
to simplify their lives, cultivate community and
spend more time with their friends and family.
www.kinfolk.com

Ouur Media is a lifestyle publisher and agency
creating print and digital media for a young
creative audience.
www.ouurmedia.com

Printed in Canada

Publication Design by Charlotte Heal
Cover Photograph by Pelle Crépin

NATHAN WILLIAMS

Editor in Chief & Creative Director

JULIE CIRELLI	**ANJA VERDUGO**
Editor	*Art Director*
JOHN CLIFFORD BURNS	**CHARLOTTE HEAL**
Deputy Editor	*Design Director*
AMY WOODROFFE	**MARIO DEPICOLZUANE**
Publishing Director	*Ouur Designer*
NATHAN TICKNOR	**DOUG BISCHOFF**
Operations Manager	*Business Operations*
JESSICA GRAY	**KATIE SEARLE-WILLIAMS**
Communications Director	*Business Manager*
PAMELA MULLINGER	**PAIGE BISCHOFF**
Advertising Director	*Accounts Payable & Receivable*
RACHEL HOLZMAN	**GEORGIA FRANCES KING**
Copy Editor	*Consulting Editor*
RACHEL EVA LIM	**CAROLYNE RAPP**
Contributing Editor	*Ouur Art Director*
MOLLY MANDELL	**SHELBY HARTNESS**
Editorial Assistant	*Art Assistant*
KELSEY BURROW	**KELSEY GLEASON**
Proofreader	*Art Assistant*
LIELA TOURÉ	**KELLY ONGKOWIDJOJO**
Marketing Assistant	*Art Assistant*
MIRUNA SORESCU	**JESSE HIESTAND**
Design Assistant	*Web Administrator*

———

SUBSCRIBE
KINFOLK IS PUBLISHED FOUR TIMES A YEAR
TO SUBSCRIBE, VISIT WWW.KINFOLK.COM/SUBSCRIBE OR EMAIL US AT SUBSCRIBE@KINFOLK.COM

CONTACT US
IF YOU HAVE QUESTIONS OR COMMENTS, WRITE TO US AT INFO@KINFOLK.COM
FOR ADVERTISING INQUIRIES, GET IN TOUCH AT ADVERTISING@KINFOLK.COM

www.kinfolk.com

arjowiggins

International standards
for creative papers

Standards internationaux
pour papiers de création

国际标准的艺术纸

Internationale Standards
für Premiumpapiere

Conqueror
Curious Collection
Keaykolour
Opale
Pop'Set
Rives
Rives Sensation
Creative Labels

Sheet sizes:
B1
1359

Arjowiggins Creative Papers
are distributed by Antalis

arjowigginscreativepapers.com

ISSUE TWENTY-ONE CONTRIBUTORS

ALEX T. ANDERSON
Writer
Seattle, Washington

PAU AVIA
Stylist
Paris, France

NEIL BEDFORD
Photographer
London, United Kingdom

SOFIE BRÜNNER
Set Designer
Copenhagen, Denmark

SARAH BUNTER
Casting Director
London, United Kingdom

KATRIN COETZER
Illustrator
Cape Town, South Africa

PELLE CRÉPIN
Photographer
London, United Kingdom

LASSE FLØDE
Photographer
Oslo, Norway

ANN MARIE GARDNER
Writer
Germantown, New York

HAGIT HADAYA
Historian
Ottawa, Canada

LILJA HRÖNN HELGADÓTTIR
Stylist
London, United Kingdom

KRISTOFER JOHNSSON
Photographer
Stockholm, Sweden

JARED KILLEEN
Writer
New York, New York

GEORGIA FRANCES KING
Writer
Brooklyn, New York

RACHEL EVA LIM
Writer
Singapore

ANDREA CODRINGTON LIPPKE
Writer
Brookhaven, New York

MOLLY MANDELL
Writer
Copenhagen, Denmark

SALLY MANN
Photographer & Writer
Lexington, Virginia

SARAH MOROZ
Writer
Paris, France

MIKKEL MORTENSEN
Photographer
Copenhagen, Denmark

HASSE NIELSEN
Photographer
Copenhagen, Denmark

CARA PARKS
Writer
New York, New York

LAURA PRAET
Prop Stylist
Ghent, Belgium

MARSÝ HILD ÞÓRSDÓTTIR
Photographer
London, United Kingdom

CAROLYNE RAPP
Stylist
Copenhagen, Denmark

MY RINGSTED
Stylist
Copenhagen, Denmark

TRISTAN RUTHERFORD
Writer
Nice, France

ANDERS SCHØNNEMANN
Photographer
Copenhagen, Denmark

SUZANNE SNIDER
Writer
New York, New York

ZOLTAN TOMBOR
Photographer
Brooklyn, New York

PIP USHER
Writer
Bangkok, Thailand

FREDERIK VERCRUYSSE
Photographer
Antwerp, Belgium

CHIDY WAYNE
Illustrator
Barcelona, Spain

NEW PERSPECTIVES ON SCANDINAVIAN DESIGN

MUUTO

New Nordic

Frame: MYKITA NO2 SUN TERESA | Photography: Mark Borthwick

MYKITA

HANDMADE IN BERLIN

WELCOME

The world's longest endurance run is the Self-Transcendence 3,100 Mile Race in Jamaica, Queens, which requires its participants to circle a single city block exactly 5,649 times—a task so demanding that few have the physical or mental endurance for it. One could say that there's a domestic analogue that happens daily inside our homes as we tread familiar routes—from the kitchen sink to the kitchen table, from the sofa to the refrigerator and back—in endless rotation. How many miles have we walked around our homes? What have we forgotten, or overlooked, in the rituals of our daily lives?

The Swedes have a name for the effects of this—*hemmablind*, literally "blind to home"—a state of having run the same route so many times, of having gazed upon the same constellation of furniture for so long, that we cease to see it. It's a concept that is explored in this issue of *Kinfolk*, along with others like it. We delve deeply into the nature of home, exploring what's hidden, overlooked, unseen, mysterious and sensual. What do we perceive of the spaces we inhabit? Do our homes have lives and characters of their own, as Indian architect B. V. Doshi asserts in *Architecture of Home*? Do ordinary objects continue their lives without us after we die, as Andrea Codrington Lippke suggests in *Memento Mori*?

Elsewhere in the issue, we take a look at the home life of reclusive pianist Glenn Gould, and author Mary Roach explores the science behind why certain places make us uneasy. Sally Mann reflects in words and photographs on the spaces where artist Cy Twombly created some of his most iconic later works, while architect Joseph Dirand, who crafts interiors for Balenciaga and Rick Owens, refuses to view his own home as a living museum and instead sprawls nightly on the carpet with his family, drawing and listening to music.

Within the pages of this issue, the home becomes more than the sum of its walls and floors, chairs and wallpaper—more than a collection of objects. The home and everything it contains are not merely ends in themselves, but the complex elements of each person's evolving and deeply personal narrative—the foundations of a well-lived life.

NATHAN WILLIAMS AND JULIE CIRELLI

Starters

The Home Issue

Starters

PHOTOGRAPH: FREDERIK VERCRUYSSE, PROP STYLIST: LAURA PRAET

WORDS
JOHN CLIFFORD BURNS

Home Blindness

When we no longer see the flaws (or strengths) in our homes, we reach a state that the Swedes call "home blind."

The old adage that chores pass unnoticed until they cease to be done neglects those segments of the home—certain surfaces or corners, perhaps even entire rooms—that remain untouched and untidied, shielded from scrutiny by some sort of force field or invisibility mirror.

Drawers, by their very nature, get full; things, as they tend to do, pile up. "Oh, it still works if you...", one might say about a door handle that requires an elaborate, secret handshake to open. Or, "You get used to it" is muttered to excuse the rattle of an AC vent, as if it were a particularly interfering aunt about whom people say, "Take no notice—that's just her way."

The Swedes use the word *hemmablind* to describe this phenomenon, which translates roughly to "home blindness." It means adapting to environments without questioning fault. We stop seeing problems to the extent that finding a solution slowly makes its way to the bottom of a to-do list until it drops off into passive acceptance.

"One could say that hemmablind is a word you would never use to describe yourself, because the moment you address something that you've become home blind to, is the moment it is no longer a matter of home blindness," explains Mark Vacher, an associate professor of ethnology at the SAXO Institute in Copenhagen, Denmark.

In that sense, home blindness exists in the murky realms of abstraction, somewhere between tacit knowledge and the past tense. It does not allow for an ambiguous grace period, unlike procrastinating doing the laundry until you've run out of clean socks, nor can it serve as an excuse: "The danger of becoming home blind is that you don't perceive the flaws or destructive patterns that you have," says Vacher. You don't *mean* to ignore the problems; you just don't see them anymore.

Vacher also extends home blindness to relationships, academia and the workplace. "It's used within business lingo as a way of detecting or talking about internal problems that have become routine to such an extent that you're all unaware of them—that's why companies hire external consultants to point out things that are counterproductive to the organization."

But it's not just the flaws we stop seeing. In fact, even if the home is just as one always hoped it would be, one can still become blind to its beauty. "A good home is a place where there aren't challenges, or where there's not even a reason to discuss them," says Vacher.

"The strength of routines and habits helps us to order the world and regard it as reliable," he continues. "And when you regard the world as reliable, you don't have to think about it—you don't have to be as alert. If you can trust your environment, then it becomes a foundation for more outgoing activities. Hemmablind allows us to go outside and meet new people, or go to the workplace and deal with challenges or problems." Taking the home for granted—regardless of leaky plumbing or impeccable interiors—actually becomes a way of defining home: If ignorance is bliss, then what better place to be blissful than at home?

WORDS
MOLLY MANDELL

Horror Vacui

—

Otherwise known as kenophobia, this Latin term expresses more than a fear of blank spaces—it's also a compulsion to fill them.

LANGUAGE: Latin

PRONUNCIATION: "Horror vack-yew-eye"

ETYMOLOGY: From *horror* meaning "fear" and *vacui* meaning "vacuum" or "empty space"

MEANING: In essence, *horror vacui* translates to "the more, the better." The phrase originated with Aristotle in connection to nature but today is typically used in reference to art and design. For Italian art critic Mario Praz, who was the first to associate the term with interior design, horror vacui conjured Victorian-era rooms crammed with elaborate combinations of furniture, fabric and colors.

USE: Horror vacui is a phrase for those at odds with the minimalist "less is more" mantra. It is not only a fear of empty space but also an uncontrollable desire to embellish it with intricate detail. Some may find an enthusiasm for patterns and polychromatic color schemes dizzying but, outside of the home, everybody experiences a little bit of horror vacui. After all, certain spaces, like the shelves that line grocery stores and libraries, are simply meant to be full.

WORDS
JULIE CIRELLI

The Big Uneasy

—

Science writer Mary Roach explores the science behind why some seemingly ordinary places give us the creeps.

Places can feel creepy for a number of reasons, many of which are not immediately obvious. Tingling spine? A strange sensation that someone is lurking just out of view? In her book *Spook: Science Tackles the Afterlife*, science writer Mary Roach explores some of the scientific theories behind why an otherwise ordinary place might feel frightening or unpleasant. In the course of her research, she came across two types of naturally occurring phenomena—electromagnetic waves and low-frequency sound waves—that are associated with feelings of unease in a place.

Among the scientists Mary interviewed for her book was neuroscience professor Michael Persinger of the Consciousness Research Lab at Laurentian University in Ontario, Canada. Persinger discovered a correlation between reported hauntings and unusually high levels of electromagnetic waves. He suspected that certain electromagnetic frequencies could trigger a condition called temporal lobe epilepsy, which causes mild seizures and can also—according to Persinger—bring on hallucinations of "an invisible, sensed presence."

To test his theory, he created a haunting chamber—a soundproof room in his lab where volunteers' brains would be plied with electromagnetic waves. Of those who volunteered to spend a few minutes in the chamber, nearly 80 percent experienced "hauntings." One saw gray, colorless figures floating along the room's perimeter; another felt her leg pulled off her body. As part of her research, Mary took a turn in the chamber. "Nothing really happened, except that I heard the 'whoop, whoop' of a police siren. I was disappointed that it wasn't more spooky—just a normal couple of whoops in a soundproof room with an orange Ski-doo helmet full of electromagnets on my head."

Next, Mary headed to Coventry University in the UK to meet with psychoacoustics researcher Vic Tandy, who theorized that there was a connection between inaudible, low-frequency sound waves called infrasound and "all manner of mysterious-seeming phenomena"—from blurred vision, "strange feelings in the stomach" and clammy skin to unexplainable bouts of emotional intensity. "Old buildings with thick walls can cause infrasound to build up," Mary explains, "This could explain why a basement might be creepier than a dentist's office."

So why, if studies point to tangible reasons why we react negatively to a place, do people often automatically reach for supernatural explanations for feelings of eeriness? "Because it's fun!" says Mary. "Don't you think it's more enticing to believe in ghosts than to believe in electromagnetic field activity or temporal lobe activity? Our lives are so ordered and explained that there's very little mystery in modern human life. This holds the door open to the unknown."

WORDS
ANN MARIE GARDNER

On Privacy

The founding editor of Modern Farmer and Monocle reflects on the intense yearning for private spaces in our homes and workplaces, and how architects and designers are starting to take note.

Our homes are beset by conflicting demands. Interior spaces must provide a sense both of community and of personal well-being; they must be places where we can invite the world in, and where we can shut the world out. In other words, they must serve needs both public and private.

In his 1953 book, *The House and the Art of Its Design*, Robert Woods Kennedy points out that design has made fewer and fewer provisions for conventional privacy, citing the example of Le Corbusier's bedroom, which contained a toilet, tub and bidet. Kennedy asks, "Where does too little privacy begin to have bad effects on the individual and the family's self-esteem? ...When the individual is not able to withdraw without undue manipulation of architectural gadgetry; without apology; and when, in emergency conditions, the family cannot operate the house according to the most conventional patterns of its time and class."

And yet, our homes don't always keep pace with our needs. The open-plan concept has been fashionable since the middle of the last century, both in urban and rural settings. Initially, it symbolized a new informality, a democratization of living areas that eliminated the distinction between formal and informal spaces, and between public and private parts of the home. In cities, this was often reflected in converted lofts and industrial buildings. In the suburbs, the artist's loft found its counterpart in the "great room"—where the kitchen, dining room and living room are combined into one shared social space.

An intense yearning for more personal space in homes and the workplace has emerged within the last five years, however. A backlash against large, multipurpose interior architecture is inspiring a move toward designing more articulated spaces, and buildings' design blueprints are starting to reflect the growing need for privacy. Some credit the shifting nature of privacy to technology—they believe we're configuring our private spaces to allow us to better curl up and tuck into a mobile device. But perhaps the move to more intimate living spaces is just the natural swinging of the pendulum.

Mary Duggan, an architect and judge for the RIBA House of the Year Award in 2015, coined the term "broken-plan homes" to describe homes that offer more walls, nooks and private spaces. But is a "broken-plan" home not simply a home as it was before the dawn of the open-plan? What sounds like a neologism reflects how architects are not simply returning to life before the open-plan, but are adapting the home in new ways.

The most innovative among them are finding creative methods for introducing more privacy. Fala Atelier in Portugal added a semicircular wall to create the illusion of seclusion in a Lisbon flat. WT Architecture added floors to break up exceptionally high ceilings in a Scottish stone mill–turned–family home. And Barcelona's Nook Architects used mesh partitions to separate the staircase from the living areas. Meanwhile, Kuwaiti firm AGi Architects created Secret House—a house that generates its own mist (on a timer) to shield the house from prying neighbors. But lower tech solutions are also available: Sliding pocket doors are now being added to close off kitchens.

These changes are also apparent in our workspaces. A report in September 2014 by office furniture specialists Steelcase found that offices without private spaces experience quantifiable problems. Losses in productivity due to lack of privacy, distracting noise and visual stimulus cost US companies up to $550 billion and UK companies up to £70 billion. But despite calls from all quarters for more privacy in the workplace, nearly 70 percent of American offices still use open-plan layouts.

Overstimulation, it seems, is robbing us of balance. In *Community and Privacy: Toward a New Architecture of Humanism*, Serge Chermayeff and Christopher Alexander write, "The very instruments that have given man increased dynamic power—total mobility and instantaneous communication—are destroying the equilibrium in the human habitat." They define the home as a protective shell, which takes a stand for us "against immediate neighbors" as it's "the only physical insulation against the dangers and pain of invasion."

However, in *The Power of Place*, Winifred Gallagher suggests that it is crowding within that protective shell—the home—that can create the ultimate stress and overstimulation. "Learning from our experiences," she writes, "can't happen unless we have refractory periods to digest them in." In other words, people need places to rejuvenate in order to absorb and process information.

Ultimately, this relationship between design and privacy becomes a human balancing act. Individuals must integrate a certain amount of solitude and a certain amount of companionship. The reintroduction of private space into the home and workplace is in fact quite optimistic. It suggests that technology might actually not take over our world. Human ingenuity may be able to provide the essential balance we crave between privacy and community.

THE ODELLS

WORDS
JOHN CLIFFORD BURNS

Architecture of Home

*Seminal Indian architect B. V. Doshi describes
the difference between a house and a home,
and how transforming the former into the
latter is a never-ending process.*

"There is a difference between a house and a home, between the product and the process," says Balkrishna Doshi. "It starts with an understanding: I'm going to make a home, so I not only want to be comfortable but I want to *feel* comfortable. I want to feel happy."

For more than half a century, Doshi has applied this simple philosophy to his work at Vastu-Shilpa, the architectural studio he founded in 1955 in Ahmedabad, India. A protégé of Le Corbusier and former associate of Louis Kahn, Doshi has created influential architecture himself; his work reads like early prototypes to the projects built by his current contemporaries—Bijoy Jain of Studio Mumbai, for example.

In blending climatic modernism with a sensory approach to and a deep understanding of vernacular craftsmanship, Doshi's buildings are largely specific to an Indian context of hot sunlight and sweeping monsoons. His "'process," however, responds to universal questions concerning the home: How do architects make people feel relaxed? What triggers a particular mood? Or, as Doshi asks, "What is the role of our eyes? Our ears? Or our skin?"

Believing that a breeze drifting through an open window or a shaft of sunlight inching across a wall might make one feel more complete than, say, a new cushion cover or kitchen appliance, Doshi subscribes to the idea that "wherever there is movement, space becomes alive."

"I believe that animation is very important in a home. A home is a character, like a living thing. Even when you remove the furniture, it tells you a story about what it is and what it wants to be. It has its own gestures."

In that sense, he says, the house should be regarded "like a growing body"—one that must "give the inhabitant freedom, choice and a feeling that, 'I can manipulate this house and use it in many ways, as and when I need'" to make it feel like home.

"I try to understand the people who are going to occupy the house and spend their life there—about the process of that life, how it operates and how it thrives and blossoms," he explains. "I want that person to feel as if the home is an extension of their life, their body and their spirit."

At Doshi's own residence—Kamala House in Ahmedabad— the blueprints have also slowly blurred into fingerprints; an extension of the architect's spirit, its form has evolved to reflect the functional needs of Doshi's family over the decades.

"In India, when you build a home, it is not meant as a temporary place—usually, it is done for people to live in for at least a generation, if not two. I designed my own house and have stayed there for the last 55 years. I added an extension—one thinks about a future when a family expands," he says. "These internal changes manifest on the outside. You see things protruding out, that things

have gone in or that certain things have become longer, shorter, bigger or smaller."

"The spaces that I design are not rigid," he continues. "My house has a staircase, a living space, a veranda and a dining room almost as one meandering room. The reason being that you can be in the garden, you can be inside, you can be on the steps or you can be isolated. You can sit on the floor, you can sit on the sofa—you can change the position of your legs and your body. We squat. We lie down. We move around."

Doshi originally built his own home according to advice that Le Corbusier, under whom he had worked in Paris during the 1950s, had personally given him: "Follow my spirit, but evolve your own way." When, later, Le Corbusier and Doshi worked together on two residences in Ahmedabad—the Shodhan and Sarabhai houses—Le Corbusier became one of Doshi's first houseguests. He told Doshi that his house "had a very nice light."

"Light has played a tremendous role in my buildings," says Doshi. "When we're sitting in a room, if we look sideways and suddenly find that there is light coming in, the psychic sense changes. I work with an idea that the quantity of light in the house should be soothing, comfortable and enjoyable."

Rather than following a conventional checklist of amenities—kitchen, bedroom, bathroom—Doshi harnesses more sensory and metaphysical properties—light, volume, climate, spatiality—to shape a building's brick and mortar; his own house is angled to catch the southwesterly breeze.

"Light and space form structure," he explains. "If there is a monsoon, you may want to sit down in one corner and experience the rain or just feel the sense of birds. As a result, you need corners, niches and places to sit around. When the sun is soft, you need to have a place to be outside. Or, when the nights are cool, could we use a terrace or a veranda to sleep or spend more time outside? That you might get birds and animals in your garden increases your sense of wonder."

Doshi's practice also applies to everyday housing—such as the projects he has designed for low-income communities in India, built with simple materials at a human scale. There, again, aside from the movement of sunlight and ventilation, each family has extended and adapted their own house independently, their homes growing and evolving much like their bodies.

"Each family has made their house their own, but the basic structure and connection to the outside remain the same," he says. "A home is not only a precious commodity. It's very much a biological order. It is very much like our Indian society: There is diversity—every house has a unique identity—but we are connected to others."

WORDS
JARED KILLEEN

Cult Rooms:
Mon Oncle

What happens when modernism becomes monstrous? The home in a classic Jacques Tati film explores how functional design can lead to domestic dysfunction.

In *Mon Oncle*, a 1958 film by Jacques Tati, the daring French parodist hangs his hat on old-fashioned European aesthetics. To illustrate the dangers of modern design, he gives us the Arpel family and their newfangled suburban home. There are no hat racks in the Villa Arpel foyer, of course, such common efficiencies having no place there. Rather, the hearth is given up for haute couture, and M. Hulot (Tati's reliably anti-modern hero) must clutch his signature bucket cap as he avoids the dangers of contemporary living.

The home in *Mon Oncle* is a Frankenstein monster of modernism, stitching together pieces of Stilnovo and Paul McCobb. The

exterior—with its dull gray façade and goggle-like upstairs windows—resembles a welder's mask. Along its perimeter runs a metal-slatted fence with an automated gate that buzzes stridently, announcing guests as if they were incorrect answers on a game show. Less lawn than obstacle course, the grounds are littered with hazards and overseen by an angry water-spewing fountain.

Inside, there's a couch that looks like chiropractic equipment and a kitchen that contains all manner of bizarre terrors: scalding burners, trapdoor cabinets and flashing panels that recall the malevolent Hal from Stanley Kubrick's *2001: A Space Odyssey*. In other words, it's a designer's

dream: chic, modern and streamlined, but completely uninhabitable. The joy of *Mon Oncle* comes in watching the Arpel family —the hapless bourgeois homeowners— mince and muddle their way through all their modern decor. Sitting in a wire chair is more like pouring yourself into a whisk. Sleeping on a lime green sofa requires first turning it on its side. Traversing the outdoor rock garden is akin to training for a varsity football team.

The Arpels are good sports, suffering quietly through the abuse. We watch them contort themselves for the sake of their brand new divan, happy to put our own feet up on the coffee table.

string®

PHOTOGRAPH: LASSE BECH MARTINUSSEN

Changing Places

---

*As home technology begins to err toward
tyranny, Marie Kristine Schmidt of Bang
& Olufsen explains how flexible designs
can lead to a more mindful mode of living.*

At the National Museum of American History, an aluminum Swanson TV dinner tray is considered a "national treasure." An unambitious object in itself, it signaled a significant social shift when introduced in 1954: Televisions usurped tables as places to gather around. Home rituals became flexible as a result of technology, as did decor.

"In the old days, you had one program and you would sit in front of the TV to watch it. The TV was very much the focal point of the living room—it basically dictated how you decorated it," says Liselotte Lyngsø, co-founder of Future Navigator, an organization for future studies in Copenhagen, Denmark. Ask where someone watches television in 2016, however, and the subtext is understood: no longer, "In which room?" but, "On which device?"

"We're designing what to watch, and when, where and how to watch it" says Lyngsø of our ability to stream, say, a missed episode of *Game of Thrones* on our tablets or smartphones—wherever we may be. But there is a tendency for technology that allows for portable home rituals to have the adverse effect—complete inertia (i.e., binge-watching in bed) and antisocial spells. "People are online all the time and have so many cyber-stimulants that we're getting new illnesses—people can't get offline," says Lyngsø, who predicts a counter-trend on the horizon: "To be more mindful around the home, more aware of what technology is doing to you."

A recent study by Danish electronics brand Bang & Olufsen showed that its subjects no longer wanted to feel tied to the technology in their pockets. "We do quite a lot of ethnographic studies where we go out and spend time in people's homes. We observe how they live, and they tell us what's important to them and their daily rhythms," says Marie Kristine Schmidt (pictured left), vice president of Bang & Olufsen. "One of the things we saw was a need for flexibility—the need for being able to move things around your house and to have a sense that you're not being dictated to."

Schmidt says that such fieldwork shapes the technology that Bang & Olufsen designs, such as its new BeoVision Horizon—a television that is mobile thanks to a set of wheels. "The question is: Do we feel all this technology is working with us, or against us? When new technology emerges, it has a tendency to complicate things rather than solve problems. The right solutions have the potential to free up time for you and bring you enjoyment in the actual interaction with the products—in a natural way that belongs to the context of the home."

Lyngsø also predicts that technology allowing for flexible living will help us regain control over our leisure time. "It allows you a more conscious living. We're already used to having these portable devices with us, but it's hard to have the willpower to turn off," she says. "It's like having a big bowl of candy sitting there—it's really hard not to eat it. But, if you can pull it out and take it away again, you can control your willpower."

Super-egg

Designed as a "useless necessity" in 1965, the brass super-egg is a classic piece of industrial art beloved by design connoisseurs.

In the early 1960s, the Danish mathematician–turned–poet Piet Hein invented the "super-ellipse," a precise geometrical cross between an oval and a rectangle. He applied his new mathematical formula to everything from a Swedish traffic hub to designs for tables and chairs and, in 1965, to the 1.5-inch-tall brass nugget he called the "super-egg."

The super-egg was a three-dimensional expression of the super-ellipse—an egg that could stand on its tip. At first, it was marketed as a thinking person's drinking game. Tip the super-egg over; if it lands on its head, drink. If it lands on its side, drink.

A booklet accompanying the super-egg listed any number of other, equally dubious applications. As an oracle, it could answer yes or no questions by landing on one side or another when tipped. As an amulet, it could boost the confidence of its owner, calm frayed nerves or reduce the temptations of cigarettes and alcohol.

Or it could do absolutely nothing. Hein readily copped to the impracticality of his beloved object—calling it "the first deliberate attempt to produce a necessity that is completely useless" and an object "unfit for any practical purpose whatsoever."

In 1969, Hein took the brass super-egg off the market permanently. Though he has since applied the super-egg formula to a number of other, more practical design objects like tables and salt-and-pepper shakers, the brass nugget has all but vanished from circulation. Today, it is a cult design object that represents the successful—if futile—quest for the perfect shape.

PHOTOGRAPH: ANDERS SCHØNNEMANN, SET DESIGN: SOFIE BRÜNNER

Amy Sall

Ahead of the launch of her new journal, editor Amy Sall reflects on her Senegalese heritage and how its physical reminders shepherd her sense of home—wherever she may be.

Decorating the sun-dappled New York City apartment of editor Amy Sall is a collection of books on African history and a poster of the film *Moolaadé* by Senegalese filmmaker Ousmane Sembène. "I give myself the right to explore anything I find interesting," Amy says. Among her social media feeds is archival and documentary imagery from Africa and the diaspora from the colonial period to the present: Grainy black-and-white footage of a 1961 meeting of the Nation of Islam appears among photos of the West African earth architecture of Mali and snapshots of Haitian street culture. Its appeal is filtered into the pages of her forthcoming journal, *SUNU: Journal of African Affairs, Critical Thought + Aesthetics.*

DO YOU HAVE A MORNING ROUTINE?

My morning routine is the same every day. I wake up and express gratitude to God, then I move to the kitchen and make myself a cup of hot water and lemon and ease into my morning. I used to be someone who checked and responded to emails immediately, but now I'm realizing that the morning is an opportunity to take your time, to set your intentions and to not succumb to any sense of urgency. Living in New York City, that sense of urgency is omnipresent and I look for ways to diminish it.

WHAT INSPIRED YOU TO START SUNU JOURNAL?

I began developing *SUNU* during my final year of grad school, in part through discussions with my mentors and peers at Columbia University. Around that time, I started to post a lot of historical and cultural images pertaining to Africa on Instagram, and people would ask questions—there would be debates, and people would comment with context for the photos. I thought it would be interesting to open up this sort of space for more dialogue. One of my inspirations is a publication called *Présence Africaine.* It was a Pan-African publishing house and quarterly publication in which notable thinkers, scholars and artists first got together to push back against colonialism by presenting their own thoughts and theories about Africa. It was started in 1947 by Alioune Diop, who was a notable professor and philosopher in Senegal. Those are the shoulders that I believe *SUNU* is standing on.

YOU WERE BORN AND RAISED IN NEW YORK BUT HAVE A CLOSE CONNECTION TO SENEGAL. WHAT TYPE OF INFLUENCE DOES THAT HAVE ON YOUR WORK?

I'm first-generation Senegalese-American and I grew up in a very Senegalese home. Growing up, I became more and more curious about Senegal—who were the great historians, who were the philosophers, who were the writers, who were the filmmakers, how the food was made. I immerse myself in Senegalese culture and history because that's something that I never want to lose. It's something I want to pass on to my own children.

WHAT IS IMPORTANT TO YOUR SENSE OF FEELING AT HOME?

I think it's important that your home makes you feel good because it's your safe space—it's your sanctuary, or at least it should be your sanctuary. I spend a lot of time at home—it's my favorite place to be—so I make sure my surroundings are comforting. I live in an apartment that gets a bit of light, but the light doesn't quite stay. I think in the future, wherever else I live, I'll want natural light throughout the day. It makes things a little better, airier and happier.

WHICH OF YOUR BELONGINGS HELP TO CREATE THAT SENSE OF SANCTUARY?

I always like to have books around me. Family photos are really important, and anything that relates to Senegal, whether it be, say, rugs, statues or other things I brought home from my travels in Senegal. Things that make me feel happy and comfortable, that's what I like to keep around.

IS THERE ONE OBJECT IN YOUR LIFE THAT YOU WOULD CONSIDER CENTRAL TO CREATING A HOME?

I'm always trying to embrace the fact that there are many sides to me. I don't ever want to have to choose one thing to represent me. But I do have special objects, one being a bracelet that I wear on my right wrist all the time. It's a Senegalese bracelet that was given to me by my parents—every time you outgrow a bracelet, your parents give you a new one. It represents my family, my culture, my country. That's one thing I would take with me no matter where I go.

Amy wears a
top and skirt
by Azede
Jean-Pierre,
vintage shoes
by Liz Claiborne
and jewelry by
Nandi Naya

Peter Jensen

———

*With designs as colorful as the muses
that influence him, Peter Jensen confronts
the fashion world with a gentle dose of
eccentricity and humor.*

If an award existed for the least fashion-y man in fashion, Peter Jensen would win every year. It's not the Dane's fondness for corduroy trousers or his longing to live in the countryside with a rabble of dogs that would score him the title—although, admittedly, they're both strong contenders. Instead, it's the fashion designer's unabashed niceness that sets him apart, and that resonates when designing clothes for a clientele he imagines to be an equally affable bunch. Ever since his first collection debuted at Paris Fashion Week in 2000, Jensen's style of eccentricity has been worn by Hollywood's most offbeat leading ladies: Kirsten Dunst, Maggie Gyllenhaal and Lena Dunham, to name a few. Beneath the obvious whimsy of playful prints, his eponymous label promotes a potent sense of individuality.

———

Looking back now, I'm really happy that I grew up in a small town in Denmark. I think it gave me ambition, drive and a longing to get out and do stuff and find myself. I had a deep fascination with British culture—the music, the art world, the fashion—and that developed when I lived in a village. I had cousins in Copenhagen and they certainly didn't have the same kind of drive—they had everything in front of them. I had to invent and search for whatever it was that I wanted to do.

An older lady who lived across the street looked after me for most of my childhood. She had no boundaries because she wasn't my mother. She never said anything about the fact that I was a boy playing with dolls. She encouraged that side of me. I played hairdressing salon with her and her elderly friends. But I have to give my mom some credit because her old sewing machine was in my bedroom. I was fascinated by it as a technical tool.

There was a girl next door who was a few years younger than me, and I made clothes for her. Every time she grew a little, we'd make something new. We were cutting things on the floor, putting them together, making them chic—or, at least, what we thought was chic. It was a really good way of learning.

The more you're away from your birth country, the more you romanticize it. I miss the Danish humor; I miss the lightness in how Danish society approaches life. I like the way Danish culture means that you can visit each other and it's okay to just stay for an hour and then leave again.

My house in London is filled with books, Danish furniture, a record player and loads of records. I like to spend hours just sitting and doing nothing. Then I'll make some doodles that come out of this boredom. I think that's what happens with my muses. Our relationships grow out of something that takes time—time to understand them, to know what you're meant to talk about and what you like about them.

All of my muses have a good story to tell. My latest muse, Peggy Guggenheim, was one of those really great women that did something with herself and her money. She was fabulous. Peggy always seemed to walk around the house in a smock dress with a fur coat on top. I like all the smock dresses in the new collection—the colors reflect the art that she collected and the clothes she dressed in.

I don't reinvent the wheel every time I do a new collection. Instead, I try to build upon what I represent within my work. I wouldn't say that I'm ever 100 percent happy when a collection is finished, but that's what drives me. Loads of my colleagues in the industry say, "This is the best thing I've ever done." I don't understand how they think like that—it's important to self-critique.

I've never fit into the fashion scene as many other people do. I'm terrible at networking. I think a lot of people have a hard time approaching me or find me cold. This makes me even more aware of the weird things I enjoy—like humor that's a bit offbeat. The one word that I really don't like being used about my collections is "quirky." I think strong women buy my stuff.

I think it's really important to have a uniform. I always wear corduroy trousers. I don't know what it is about them, but I think they suit my body and who I am as a person and they make me happy. You know how you can put things on and they make you feel right? Corduroy trousers do that for me.

My plan is to keep doing what I do, and make some serious money out of it and retire in 10 years' time. I'd like to have a house in Denmark and another in the English countryside. Then I will learn to drive, get a few more dogs, cook—though I can't cook at all at the moment, nor drive. Then I will throw big dinner parties and organize them in the most glamorous way.

PHOTOGRAPH: MARSÝ HILD ÞÓRSDÓTTIR. STYLING: LILJA HRÖNN HELGADÓTTIR

Peter wears a
sweater by Acne
Studios and a
shirt of his own
design

Hikari Yokoyama

With her impeccable eye and sense of entrepreneurialism, Hikari Yokoyama is charting her own course through the contemporary art world.

Raised in the Midwest with a Bahá'í-guided detachment toward material culture, Hikari Yokoyama has honed her sense of impartiality as a consultant within the contemporary art world. Whether connecting brands for collaboration, building companies such as Paddle8—the online auction house she co-founded—or serving on the board of Women for Women International, Hikari excels at bringing projects to life.

HOW DO YOU DESCRIBE WHAT YOU DO FOR A LIVING?

I've always been a bridge person. In art school, I realized very quickly that I wasn't yearning to say something through my own work—that I didn't have to make work—I preferred learning what others had to say. I'm interested in figuring out ways to present ideas to different audiences, often through the medium of art. While I respect the art world, I'm more interested in speaking to those who are not necessarily inside the coven—creating pathways that allow people to engage in different ways, get excited or have a deeper understanding. I also quite enjoy the challenge of opening closed minds.

WHAT TYPES OF PROJECTS ALLOW YOU TO DO THAT?

I frame information into doors for people to walk through—such as when we started our personality-driven sales on Paddle8 that gave people insight into art through the eyes of others. Or our dossiers, when we would pick an individual artwork and mind map information around it in the form of a web page. I also recently gave a talk for French fragrance line By Kilian, where I connected complex smells to master works of art. And I look forward to working with Gucci at the Frieze Masters Talks each year, when one artist speaks about another artist's work. It's like gossip for ideas—speaking about someone else's work reveals more about their own character and values.

DO PEOPLE OFTEN MISTAKE YOUR WORK FOR CURATION? WHAT DO YOU THINK THAT TERM MEANS TODAY?

I've worked as a curator for various projects, and I've worked with curators as well. The traditional definition is a highly trained professional who presents exhibitions to the public, usually working for a museum or a gallery. In the age of information saturation, this word is often borrowed and applied to all sorts of scenarios—it's a word that simultaneously has become more relevant and also more ambiguous. If you wanted to be pedantic, you could even say you have to curate your fridge every time you go to the grocery store.

WHICH ASPECTS OF YOUR WORK ARE MOST MEANINGFUL TO YOU?

I go through ebbs and flows of zooming out, looking at all of my work and asking myself this same question. At times, I can feel that it's not that meaningful—I think, I am not engineering bridges or inventing the light bulb or performing eye surgeries on children. But then I remember that the freedom of expression that we have through the arts is a privilege not to be taken for granted. Without art, I don't think it's possible to really have an understanding of what it means to be human. Many peo-

PHOTOGRAPH: MARSÝ HILD ÞÓRSDÓTTIR. STYLING: LILJA HRÖNN HELGADÓTTIR

Hikari wears
a blazer by Rejina
Pyo, bangle by
Maria Black, double
ring by URiBE and
her own silver rings.

Hikari wears a
top by Freya
Dalsjø.

PHOTOGRAPH: MARSÝ HILD ÞÓRSDÓTTIR, STYLING: LILJA HRÖNN HELGADÓTTIR

ple alive today are prohibited from creating freely and openly. I've also carved out a way of doing more grounded work as a trustee of Women for Women International. We work to empower women from conflict zones to build a better life for themselves. I've personally had enough of women not being afforded their human rights and, like any social movement, the only way the situation can change is from within. Women around the world must work together to help everyone along. This work is much more nuanced and important than anything that could be represented by a financial figure.

HOW DIFFERENT WOULD YOUR CAREER BE WITHOUT THE INTERNET?

That is very much the counterfactual conditional, as my philosopher friend would say. It's difficult to imagine what the world would be like if there were no internet—it's now a significant portion of my brain. I no longer need to remember bits of information, but I can remember how to access them through keywords or folder names. I think the next phase of human development is going to be balancing the flow of information that machines constantly give us with our human physiology that yearns for more than just efficiency at any cost.

WHAT WAS THE LAST THING YOU MADE WITH YOUR HANDS?

A ceramic pot I made on a wheel at Antony Gormley and Vicken Parsons' house.

WHAT TYPE OF OBJECTS DO YOU LIKE TO BE SURROUNDED BY AT HOME?

I change a lot, but right now I want to rid myself of anything extraneous. I want to have only what's essential and the best of that. I love decadence, but I hate waste. I believe that objects can hold energies, and even how they look can influence how you think about the world around you. Some inanimate objects can be like a jolt of lightning to your psyche day after day, while some fade in power quite quickly. I want to have things made with integrity and objects that serve the clearest function.

ARE YOU WHERE YOU WANTED TO BE AT THIS STAGE IN YOUR LIFE?

I've never really wanted to be in any place other than exactly where I am right now. I don't think of life as stages, either, but rather as one long unraveling, meandering, unpredictable exploration of self and the wider world. I certainly have a vision of where I would like to go and what I would like to be, but this fluctuates as I move through the current moment—it's not a fixed visualization. I've always envied people who knew right away exactly what they wanted to do but I've always resonated with the idiom that cats have nine lives.

HOW WOULD YOU DESCRIBE YOUR CHILDHOOD?

My upbringing was very strange. I grew up completely normal in the sense of the middle-class American dream of the late 20th century—I went to a good school that was free, and I had a bicycle that allowed me to roam around my neighborhood until I had to be home by sunset. I did all the things that people around me did, like play on the soccer team and go trick-or-treating. But I was also always an outsider and never fit in completely with the Midwestern way of life.

HOW SO?

I was half Japanese and half Bahá'í, my father being from Japan and my mother devout. I was living by this relatively young Persian religion that no one around me had ever heard of. In the years when conspicuous consumption was cool, I was being taught detachment and not to be materialistic. I didn't fit in with my parents either—they both had conflicting visions of what a "successful person" looks like. I love them both, but I had to go out into the world to seek my own identity.

SO WHAT HAS SUCCESS COME TO MEAN TO YOU?

For me, success is being able to do things with integrity, having the freedom to take risks and not feeling inhibited by the logistics of life.

Home

WORDS
SARAH MOROZ

PHOTOGRAPHS
LASSE FLØDE

STYLING
PAU AVIA

French architect Joseph Dirand acquired his first Prouvé chair at the tender age of 17 and has favored function over form ever since. Now he's creating his own kind of minimalism and injecting his signature Parisian sangfroid into interiors for Rick Owens and Balenciaga. Here he discusses his architectural icons Carlo Scarpa and Mies van der Rohe, his predilection for techno and Land Art and his lack of pretense at home with family.

New Minimalist
Joseph Dirand

Joseph Dirand's stark design articulates the sumptuous essentials. His aesthetic is wielded through a serenely—and masterfully—scaled-down approach. Slender and garrulous, the Parisian born-and-raised architect delivers French opulence with great restraint, accentuating both the past and the ultramodern for projects within his country (the Rosenblum Collection in Paris, the Villa Pierquin in Saint Girons), as well as exporting his finesse to places like the Saifi Penthouse in Beirut and the Distrito Capital hotel in Mexico.

His professional headquarters in Paris' 9th arrondissement—where he was interviewed—is a luminous sixth-floor perch on the Right Bank with an unobstructed view over the city's rooftops. The open-plan workspace for his staff of 25 is trimmed with neatly arranged groupings of every kind of material sample, and his personal office is equipped with a full library of art and architecture books and his favorite Jeanneret chair.

Dirand readily discusses his architectural icons, including Carlo Scarpa and Mies van der Rohe, but slips just as easily into his predilection for techno and his fondness for Land Art. During the interview, Dirand often runs his fingers through his salt-and-pepper hair, and briskly strokes at his stubble—the only twitches to his otherwise polished command of who he is and what he does with his striking visual vocabulary.

He has always been attracted to minimalism, likely a reactionary pivot from the context in which he grew up. His mother was a fashion designer; she loved flea markets and sourcing vintage things. His father was a successful architectural and interiors photographer (notably working for *The World of Interiors*). He photographed something very different nearly every day. Dirand accompanied his father on shoots, even assisting him at times.

"It was a lot of information, great culture, but it was also a bit of a hodgepodge. I couldn't really create my own sensibility through the amount of things I was receiving." The wealth of experiences could tip into a sense of oversaturation and chaos, influencing Dirand's attraction toward the ultimate in reduction and simplicity.

The house he was raised in was an old dance studio in Paris, a glass and metal structure from the 1930s. The family home had "no two chairs the same," recalls Dirand—think a plush red velvet seat next to a rustic farmhouse chair. "It's great… but I cannot live like that!" he laughs. "My father changed his tastes every day, basically." Consequentially, Dirand's own tastes became about "erasing everything and starting from a blank page."

His father always wanted to be an architect—it was one of his passions—but never studied the discipline. That single-minded desire was passed down to his son; Dirand remembers, as early as age 12, writing a book on Le Corbusier.

"On holidays, we were frequently going to see buildings in different cities," he recalls, amused. He bought his first Prouvé chair at age 17 at a flea market for 600 francs. That chair would be valued at almost $17,000 now. By age 21, Dirand was designing small-scale apartments for friends of the family in tandem with his studies at École Nationale Supérieure d'Architecture Paris-

Joseph Dirand

"My design is not only about a certain look. It is about life. People will sit next to each other, work at the table, have sex; it will be amazing. All of this is important."

Joseph Dirand

Joseph Dirand

Belleville. These experiences provided a robust enough start that it enabled him to open his eponymous studio straight after graduation, in 1999.

Over the past nearly two decades, his studio has become ever more in demand. One of his specialties is creating spectacular settings in service of diverse luxury labels. When Balmain called upon him to design the Paris flagship boutique, he delivered something "very classic 18th-century." Dirand explains: "I was working on a brand that has this heritage of haute couture that needed to be respected—because when you have a story, it's nice to keep and continue it." He describes the chosen aesthetic as "very abstract, very modern, very Kubrick-feeling."

When it came time for a sister boutique in London, he translated the French 18th-century fixtures into something location-appropriate, with modified ceilings, floors and typography that had an 18th-century English infusion. "But it's the same mood," Dirand emphasizes. "Like Balmain's holiday home."

Balmain is just one of many luxury labels he's designed for. "Pucci and Rick Owens are so different: One is glamorous, the other is Brutalist," he says, citing other examples of his high-end clientele. (Balenciaga, Givenchy and Alexander Wang boutiques are also among his portfolio.) "It was an amazing exercise for me to be able to source and create scenarios that link what these labels do with what they think and with who they are physically." Although it can be tricky to work with competitors, he entirely reinvents shapes, proportions and styles to match each client. "The most important element is that it's coherent with the brand: what it is, where it was."

All of Dirand's designs start with references from movie scenes, books and other iconic designers. When he launches a project, he begins by revisiting his own bookshelf. For a new building in LA, he's been consulting photographs by Ed Ruscha to get a time-specific vision of modernism. For a project in the Bahamas, his inspiration for a set of colonial-style bungalows is an adaptation of traditional Japanese dwellings.

Digital research is, inescapably, an influence too: "Google is my best friend; we are all addicted and on it for hours. It opens doors and doors and doors," he concedes.

Today, Dirand delves into new projects that are novel, relative to his repertoire. "I'm trying not to repeat myself, so it will be very hard for me to design a bourgeois apartment in Paris. I have no interest in that now," he states. That said, he acquiesces: "I will always do residential projects when they are ambitious." Such opportunities

allow for innovations—and munificence in terms of cost, time and complexity—that can only be deployed in the private sector.

Still, Dirand has mostly shifted from commercial boutiques and individual residences to hospitality and entire buildings. He recently inaugurated Loulou, the airily elegant restaurant nestled in Paris' Musée des Arts Décoratifs, and has already won accolades for his restaurant Monsieur Bleu, whose velvet banquettes and marble-and-oak floors are housed within the Palais de Tokyo contemporary art museum across town.

"It's giving me an opportunity to share my work," he reasons of wanting a bigger reach and more frequented places. "I have stores I designed that don't exist anymore. Brands change, locations change… I have more ambition to create venues that will last for a really long time and create strong memories for people."

Currently, he is working on a Four Seasons hotel that will open in Miami. When tackling a new place, he addresses the contextual clichés head-on. For Miami, he free-formed with "vulgar but chic but glamorous but '50s… Art deco, pastel colors, palm trees, turquoise water, clouded sky." The resulting deluxe suites cleverly emphasize the building's astonishing waterside view through the careful placement of five-foot mirrors, which in turn seemingly change the proportions of the rooms.

"You really gain something," he says of this decision. (In the bathrooms, he also incorporated mirrors that enable a view of the sea from the showers.) Dirand conceived of L-shaped travertine stone cushioned daybeds—"almost the same color as the sand, for continuity"—that guests can build their stay around. "This is not only about a certain look. It is about life," he says of his design. "People will sit next to each other, work at the table, have sex; it will be amazing. All this is important," he stresses. In this way, Dirand truly thinks cinematographically: about movement, about how one circulates in space and the experiences within it.

"I work a lot with contrast to create a sense of depth—it allows me to play with space and light, with perspective," he says. His attentive sense of framing, geometry and luminosity is the kind of expertise that turns him into a spatial magician. "For me, good architecture pleases you when you see it for the first time, but right after disappears into amazing moments."

Dirand's thoroughly experiential approach means he's involved in aspects well beyond the scope of the mise-en-scène of a room: He reviews the logo, the website, the playlist corresponding to the spaces he works on. He tastes the food with the chef at the restaurant; he does complete mock-ups of suites and tests the bed for hotels.

"I wouldn't do a restaurant for someone who doesn't know how to do food. Because even if I do the most incredible architecture, if the food is bad, my project will be a bad experience." He equates his exacting approach with a dandy's sense of meticulousness. A dandy, he remarks, "has style, but he has his own style, and he pays attention to every single detail in his life, aesthetically, to create a beautiful life. He cares about everything." To maintain such

---

an integral vision, "we work with visionary people," he says. "We are living at a time when risk is something people don't like; they only copy what's been done before. Developers will spend this, because they know, in this area, it will sell that. A visionary can say: 'Yeah, but maybe there are people who will be happy to pay more to have something much better.'" Dirand continues: "It's important to collaborate with people who are driving the project exactly the same way you are driving it. Little by little you find those people, and you work with them again. And then you almost don't need any other clients."

Such great partnerships are knitted together through a mutually liberal and trusting spirit. "I need to love my client, and for them to love me as well," he says. "Selectivity means you work with people who give you more freedom, who give you the opportunity to develop extraordinary things." In order to feel suitably devoted to these long-term projects that take many years to realize, he has to want to invest his whole life into the process.

"The rhythm is very extreme," he notes of the commitment, the travel and the ceaseless finessing. Moreover, he says, "I need people who challenge me—I like when my clients are difficult with me, exigent, so if I sometimes feel a little lazy, they will reawaken me." Reawakenings are crucial to the design process, as Dirand feels that "you can reinvent something again and again—there's always something to improve, even in functionality."

With his team, he says: "We love when it's difficult. We love to prototype—we want to design everything: the handle of the door, the taps, we are even thinking of working with brands to customize fridges. You need to find challenges that force you to go further and further and explore and be amazed by the result. We do it until we get every proportion right, every color." He continues: "The more you do, the more it will open your appetite. And if you don't like it, you change it."

To preserve such a high standard, "We work with the best craftsmen on the planet—who just happen to be French," he laughs. "We are such an old culture that the savoir faire has been transmitted from generation to generation. We haven't lost from the past, but we gain from the new."

Very much like the artisanal skills he cites, honed over centuries, Dirand values durability and longevity. Instead of building a generic white concrete building, he advocates for gorgeous stone. "It's not just expensive for the sake of being expensive: A stone building is something that will be even more beautiful in a century, whereas the other building will look ugly in 10 years," he states. His rigor about quality informs the clientele he attracts: "I prefer to know that my clients—my community—will be sensitive to where they're going to live. That's what I care about."

Surprisingly, when it comes to his own living arrangement, Dirand is renting. "But I destroyed everything; I did six months of heavy work, redoing the windows, the ceiling, the floor, the heating system." As he and his partner each have a daughter, "I had to find a place where I was able to host two little girls, and design a

Joseph Dirand

"We are not precious. My objects are, but I don't treat them as though they were. If something breaks it breaks; but they're only objects, in the end."

Joseph Dirand

Dirand recently
inaugurated Loulou,
a restaurant located in
Paris' Musée des Arts
Décoratifs

Joseph Dirand

space specifically for our lives." The children are with the couple every other week, and Dirand wanted something that "doesn't feel empty when they're not there." He is very underwhelmed by Paris' ubiquitous neo-classical Haussmannian buildings—instead, his residence is in a 17th-century *hôtel particulier* on the Left Bank. The renovated 2,000-square-foot space in the 7th arrondissement showcases a beautiful staircase and entrance hall, 12-foot ceilings, Versailles-style parquet floors with a heating system below the boards, curved cornices and every wall done in marmorino plaster. "You have the technology, the comfort and the beauty of the materials," he says proudly of his home. "It's a piano nobile."

Dirand has moved three times in his life, and each time, he says, "I've kept the objects that I love. I continue to buy, but the base is perfect. Everything at home is a collected piece: every ceramic, every ashtray." He rarely changes the decor of his home. Although he's set in his layout, "I don't want to live in a museum—it has to be friendly," he adds. "Our girls"—ages four and nine—"are jumping around. It's a happy home. We are not precious—my objects are, but I don't act with them as though they were. If something breaks it breaks; they're only objects, in the end." Moreover, he insists: "I cannot compromise comfort for beauty." Beautiful items that are nonfunctional are simply considered sculpture.

Dirand collects art as well as design, and regularly attends fairs and galleries. His tastes lean, naturally, toward minimalism and Arte Povera–inflected pieces. He collects artists such as Sterling Ruby, Jacob Kassay and Lawrence Carroll; he recently bought work by Sergej Jensen and Jannis Kounellis ("Another Alfabeto—I'm addicted," he confesses). "A good piece will always increase in value—and if you don't sell the piece, you don't care," he reasons.

His rituals at home—aside from carrot juice in the morning—are about working alongside his partner, Anne-Sophie Bilet, the creative director of his restaurants and a DJ. "She mixes and I design. We are so concentrated on what we do that we are together, but not together." He elaborates: "We stay up late in the living room, me on the carpet at a very low table, drawing. All of my projects have been conceived sitting on the carpet working with transparent paper. I come back to the office with them"—he pulls out a box and rustles through a pile to demonstrate—"and at the same time, Anne-Sophie is sourcing music and mixing."

Though they frequently travel, both for work and for pleasure, Dirand says: "The space that we prefer most on earth is our home." For him, "A house inspires you and makes you the way you are." He notes: "I have done houses for people that have changed their aesthetic, their lifestyle and their expectations. If you are with your kids, and before you were sitting in front of a wall, while now you are sitting around together, more comfortably, so the kids can play… everything is here to create a proper life."

Dirand has never studied feng shui, "but I'm sure that what we do is feng shui—because feng shui is, in a way, brightness in interiors." Or as he otherwise puts it, "Design needs to be generous—you create moments of life. You create pleasure."

"We stay up late in the living room, me on the carpet at a very low table, drawing. All of my projects have been conceived sitting on the carpet working on transparent paper."

Left: Dirand's tastes in art and design lean toward minimalism and Arte Povera–inflected pieces. But, he says, "I cannot compromise comfort for beauty." For Dirand, beautiful items that are nonfunctional are simply considered sculpture.

WORDS
MOLLY MANDELL

PHOTOGRAPHS
HASSE NIELSEN

STYLIST
MY RINGSTED

Object

Matters

Long Europe's design capital, Copenhagen is the source of some of the world's most innovative and beautiful design objects. We asked eight of the city's creative leaders to share the stories behind their most precious possessions, from a teapot designed by Henning Koppel to a wooden bowl from Germany and a Spanish guitar.

SILAS ADLER—Co-founder and creative director of Danish fashion brand Soulland Silas Adler lusted after Marcel Breuer's Wassily Chair long before his girlfriend gave it to him as a housewarming gift. In Silas' home, the chair not only serves as an iconic Bauhaus piece but has also become a refuge. "Our home isn't full of clutter so it feels like everything really has its place and gets a lot of attention. For me, the chair has become a spot where you can reflect because you can't see the TV from it. Obviously, you can sit on it and look at your phone, but it's more of a place where you take a book, sit down and try to focus. That's really what I love about it."

KWAMIE LIV — Musician Kwamie Liv's belongings are reflective of the two constants in her life—travel and music—so it comes as no surprise that her instruments are some of her most prized possessions. She has two guitars—a Spanish guitar that she has owned since childhood and a western guitar gifted to her by a close friend. "They both carry their own stories and have followed me all over the place. The thing that I like about them is that they move. I like the fact that even though where I live or the space I'm in might change, I can carry them with me and still use them to create, which is the essence of what makes me happy."

MALENE MALLING — Publisher Malene Malling doesn't believe in saving precious belongings, such as her Henning Koppel teapot, for special occasions. "I think you should bring the beauty into your everyday life and treasure it. Even though it's a bit of a pricey piece, it gives me pleasure every day." The teapot, designed for Georg Jensen, also emphasizes the brightness of her home. "When you grow up in Scandinavia, light is important because you have so little of it. I think one of the most beautiful things is when you have windows on both sides of a building and get a lot of light in a room. The silver teapot has the effect of reflecting light beautifully."

DORTE MANDRUP — Architect Dorte Mandrup rarely feels a deep connection to any of her possessions, but a turquoise Saxbo vase designed by Eva Stæhr Nielsen in the '50s is an exception. "It's part of Danish design history but it's also a part of who I am. I'm not so attached to objects. I don't care when I move from one apartment to another, but I really like to have this object with me." The vase was originally a wedding present for Dorte's parents, but her mother gave it to her when she moved away from her childhood home. It has followed her ever since. "It's a really lovely piece because it's timeless. It's classic, yet still very modern."

KRISTOFFER SAKURAI — In his previous home, the founder of Sakurai Creative Vision typically stayed away from furniture made of light wood. Now, one of his most treasured belongings is an oak bench made in collaboration with Belgian producer St-Paul Home. "It's sandy colored with tones of gray and beige. It goes perfectly with the surroundings of our house, which is very close to the beach and to the forest." It is paramount that the objects in his home reflect their setting. "I think it's very important that when you create a home, you create that home out of who you are, the personalities that you have and your own personal taste and style. But it's also very important that you look at your surroundings, that you look at where you are."

JOACHIM KORNBEK HANSEN — As the design and brand manager of Danish interiors company Menu, it's natural that Joachim Kornbek Hansen's furniture would take center stage in his home. "I want my apartment to be a frame so that the furniture is like the painting." A particularly iconic item in his home is Menu's red Afteroom chair. "I think it shows the simplicity and sophisticated elegance that I often appreciate in furniture." When he ordered it in red, he didn't predict what would follow. "I wanted it for my new home, but one of the women who puts things into the system at Menu thought it was part of the collection. It was meant as a personal customized item for me, but it ended up as part of Menu's collection."

ERIC LANDON — Ceramicist and co-founder of Danish ceramics studio Tortus, Eric Landon seeks objects that, just like his own work, are a labor of love. A favorite of his is a bowl by German woodworker Hendrick Hendricks. "It's absolutely perfect in the forming and in the finish. I like objects that really show the dedication and the heart of the craftsman. I think it's easy to spot things that are made in that spirit." Eric is intrigued by more than just appearance, however. "That's one of the rules we have in our home. We don't have anything that we don't use. It's important that the things we have, even if they're decorative, still play a functional role. I think that's where aesthetics and living really fit together."

YVONNE KONÉ — Accessories designer Yvonne Koné prefers simplicity in her home, frequently getting rid of unnecessary belongings. When she reflects on her favorite items, two West African hairdresser signs come to mind. "They are simple and very honest. They say, 'This is what you'll get. There are not many options.'" Though the signs are among her oldest possessions, she did once try to throw them away. Unbeknownst to Yvonne, her husband saved them. "We've only moved twice since then, but I don't feel like throwing them out anymore. Sometimes they are given a new space, but they are little signs that this is my home. At the moment, one of them is hanging in my youngest son's room."

Untitled (Window with Helmets), 2012

From *Remembered Light* at Gagosian Gallery

Gelatin Silver Print, 8 x 10 inches

Edition of 5

REMEMBERED LIGHT

In her memoir Hold Still, photographer Sally Mann wrote of the "tinge of sorrow" that permeates life in Lexington, Virginia, the sleepy Southern town where Mann created her most iconic images and where she and the artist Cy Twombly were friends and confidants for more than 20 years. Here Mann writes intimately of her relationship with Twombly and the photographs she made of his studio before his death in 2011, now on view at Gagosian Gallery in New York in the exhibition Remembered Light.

The older you get as an artist the higher the risks of success. The more work that surrounds a career, the more likely that the entrapment of past production will constrict future work, tying us ever more tightly to our style, our themes, our aesthetic past.

For example, when I was just starting out as an artist, I'd take pictures of anything, just for the sheer joy of seeing what it looked like as a photograph. Over time I began to take pictures of subjects that I had an opinion about, or of subjects that illuminated an intellectual concept that interested me. I don't mean I was illustrating a polemic; I always defer to the imperatives of beauty, lyricism and the universal resonance of felicitous proportion. But, all the same, much of my work is in service to a concept: the nature of childhood, of family, the haunted nature of the Southern landscape, death and so on.

But Cy approached art-making somewhat differently, and his rapturous delight in all things colorful (or marmoreally white), in all that was vital, wacky, elegant or inelegant in his daily passage through life came to infect me—and it was a most welcome contagion. So when I happened by his studio one day with a few sheets of color film left from a trip to Mexico, I took a few snaps for the hell of it. To see what they looked like. Just like the old days. And it went from there... whatever camera I happened to have in the car at the time, whatever film was in it—I took casual, fast, easy snaps. No pressure, no agenda and certainly no exhibition in mind—just a tender, fun and casual embrace of Cy's working world.

Interestingly, during the course of what I now realize is a narrative exploration of the evolution of a work space, I evolved from 8x10 color and black-and-white film to color digital and finally back to the same materials with which I started photography in 1968: 35mm Tri-X film in my ancient (even then) Leica. I think it was Cy's influence that liberated me from the trap

"I was never particularly interested in having Cy himself in the pictures—he was there in spirit. And what a spirit it was. Audacious yet courtly, and always perfectly mannered."

of my view camera and allowed me to begin messing around with different media, different cameras, different film. And of course I didn't care that the fluorescents screwed up the color balance, just as Cy himself didn't care about any of the manifold issues in the place—the great gashes of western sun streaming in, the impossibility of unimpeded movement. It was just fun, snapping away, or, in his case, loopily painting under those humming green bulbs. I was never particularly interested in having Cy himself in the pictures—he was there in spirit. And what a spirit it was. Audacious and yet courtly, always perfectly mannered. Soft-spoken, almost shy, but bold in his gaze, occasionally withering in his contempt or censure (as when he scolded me for an over-exuberant recitation of some miscreant behavior that I found hilarious). By turns embarrassed by the bawdy and delighted by it. Occasionally dismissive and grumpy, imperious at moments, but tender and sweet at others. Kind of like the rest of us, actually. Only bigger and better and smarter and more audacious and altogether magisterial.

I wish my parents were around still to tell me what he had been like as a kid. They had known him since he was a teen, and Cy once brought them a little sweetie of a sculpture as a thank-you for having him to dinner (I told you he was well-mannered). But my mature relationship with him only began when I was in my late 30s, so by then he was pretty well-formed.

But, in a certain sense, he was not fully Cy even then. He was mustering his resources, gathering his strength for what turned out to be a last, extravagantly successful artistic homestretch sprint. I'm not a Twombly scholar and I hesitate to suggest his emotional motivations, but I had the impression that he had been hurt by his past experiences in the American art world, finding Europe more welcoming. I am not entirely sure he came back to Lexington to make work, but once he got started in that warehouse across from our home, he began a steady acceleration into the final romp to the finish.

In *Hold Still*, I make a big deal about the importance of the South and its ineffable quiddities and seductions, its artistic impossibilities and imperatives. Who the hell knows if my theories are correct about Cy and why he, too, loved the South. I know why I love it and derive such inspiration from it and, naturally, want to assume that he felt the same way I do about it. He certainly had many of the personal hallmarks of a Southerner and his work, I feel, reflected the much-cherished (in the South) and innately contradictory qualities of ambiguity and plainspokenness, cruelty and kindness, illumination and obscurity.

Like all Southerners, he was keenly aware of the omnipresence of death, but the shadow of mortality failed to darken his brilliance, and the famous slow pace of Southern life only served to remind Cy of how much harder he needed to work.

Remembered Light*, an exhibition of Sally Mann's portraits of Cy Twombly's studio, is on view at Gagosian Gallery in New York.*

Untitled (Dancing Cherubs), 2011/2012
From *Remembered Light* at Gagosian Gallery
Platinum Print, 9 x 14 inches
Edition of 3

Untitled (Angled Light), 1999-2000

From *Remembered Light* at Gagosian Gallery

Gelatin Silver Print, 20 x 24 inches

Edition of 3

Untitled (Pencil Painting), 1999-2000
From *Remembered Light* at Gagosian Gallery
Gelatin Silver Print, 16 x 20 inches
Edition of 5

PHOTOGRAPHS
PELLE CRÉPIN

STYLING
CAROLYNE RAPP

CASTING
SARAH BUNTER

Modern
Movement

With its clean lines, high ceilings and ample use of natural materials, Emmanuel de Bayser's apartment in Berlin is the epitome of modernist living. His eclectic mix of furniture, including pieces by Charlotte Perriand and Pierre Jeanneret, inspires a sartorial silhouette that's equal parts muted and bright.

CHARLOTTE
PERRIAND

Un art d'habiter

The STORY of EAMES FURNITURE

Jean Royère

Galerie Jacques Lacoste · Galerie Patrick Seguin

DAVID BOWIE IS INSIDE

HITCHCOCK/TRUFFAUT

VISCONTI
Bruno Villien

PIER PAOLO PASOLINI

Muriel TINEL
Martine BOYER

DES HOTELS & DES ILES

VACANCES ROYALES

ASPEN
THE SPIRIT OF

HAMPTONS
THE SPIRIT OF

She wears trousers
by COS and shoes
by Robert Clergerie.
Bowl by Alexandre
Noll and ceramics
by Georges Jouve

The co-owner of fashion boutique The Corner Berlin was drawn to the 19th-century building for its sense of peace, solidity and timelessness. Table and chair by Jean Prouvé (left) and chair by Pierre Jeanneret (right)

Left: She wears a top by J.W.Anderson, skirt by Mafalda von Hessen and shoes by Gucci. This page: Bag by Saint Laurent, bowl by Suzanne Ramié and table and chair by Jean Prouvé

This page: Ceramics
by Pol Chambost and
Georges Jouve. Right:
She wears a dress by
Peter Jensen and shoes
by Céline

She wears a dress by
Peter Jensen. Sofa by
Jean Royère, ceramics
by Georges Jouve,
table, shelf and stools by
Charlotte Perriand

This page: She wears a
top by Rick Owens and
trousers by COS. Right:
Bag by Loewe, chair by
Pierre Jeanneret, lamp
by Gino Sarfatti and
table by Jean Prouvé

de agostino color. Special thanks to The Corner Berlin and Peter Jensen for providing the clothing for the shoot

IN CONVERSATION:

THE COMMODIFICATION OF HOME

————

INTERVIEW BY GEORGIA FRANCES KING

If houses are the physical manifestations of personalities, what does it mean for our domestic lives when we begin to turn our homes into businesses? Through curating them as the backdrop to personal brands or using them as a once-in-a-blue-moon rental revenue stream, we've now come to commodify our living spaces. To learn more about this tug-of-war between our authentic and ideal homes, we spoke to social scientists Sam Gosling and Lindsay Graham about what happens when our private lives go public, whether we're conscious of it or not.

Please describe what you do and your main fields of study.
SAM: I'm a professor of psychology at the University of Texas at Austin, and I study the connections between people and places, both how we affect the spaces around us and how those spaces affect us. I've also done quite a lot of work on personality in animals, and I also work on developing new methods to collect data in behavioral sciences—how we can use smartphones to learn about how people behave, for example.

LINDSAY: I'm a researcher at the University of California, Berkeley, and the Center for the Built Environment. I study how people express themselves through space and modify their environments to best fit their daily lives in both virtual and physical spaces. My work also focuses on how components of the indoor environment can be modified to affect people both positively and negatively, and what impact this has on how people formulate their identities.

To what extent have we started to commodify our homes?

SAM: The home has been a commodity for a long time, in a sense, because we've always used it as a place for entertaining others. We have spaces in our houses that nobody but very intimate others come into, then there are semi-public spaces that serve as a forum for presenting your values, your identity and what's important to you—your cultural associations, your religious associations and so on. The audience might be brought into our living rooms in a slightly different manner now, but I'm not sure that it's a hugely radical shift.

LINDSAY: I agree and disagree. Homes have long been spaces where we connect with others. We use them to welcome people and to make them feel connected to us. What's interesting is that now we're opening our homes in quite different ways than we did in the past—the idea that your home might be opened up to somebody aside from yourself or your close others is a really big shift. Until recently, our homes have been perceived as these safe havens and private spaces, but that's changing in some ways as we open them up to strangers.

The only people who used to see the insides of our homes were those we let in through the front door, but now that we've begun projecting our homes on social media, the entirety of the internet might be looking at our curtains. How is social media impacting the way we display our identities through our homes?

LINDSAY: I've been thinking about this a lot lately. Social media has broken down barriers that we have about sharing ourselves—we let others see these really intimate parts of our lives now. We're in this mode of expressing who we are without filters, which causes us to think more about how others perceive us. I've been at many social gatherings where the stage has to be set before we take a photo—all the mess on the dining table has to be moved to make the shot look nice. There's an awareness that people have now that they didn't before.

SAM: There are various ways in which we seek to express ourselves to others, and in a sense, social media is just another channel. As new forms of expression show up, we make use of them to express our identity. When we have cars, we put bumper stickers on them. When we have email, we put signatures at the bottom. People are happier, healthier and more productive when they can bring others to see them as they see themselves.

Why is there an obsession with authenticity and appearing perfectly imperfect?

LINDSAY: Sam and I have spent a lot of time talking about personality in relationship to this topic. There's this image within our culture right now that you want to appear "real" and down to earth—and part of that is manufacturing realness as well.

SAM: If you want people to think that what you project is a true reflection of who you are in terms of your goals, your ideals, your behaviors and the emotions you feel, it doesn't work if it seems to be staged. If it looks deliberately tousled, then it's no better than it being deliberately perfect.

But doesn't the fact that we're clearing the dirty plates off the dinner table before taking that photograph make the entire thing inauthentic?

LINDSAY: Sam and several others have done work that's looked at whether we are authentically presenting ourselves within those social forums, and the evidence has shown that we are. We have really strong identity claims that we strive to be associated with, and we want to be seen as possessing certain characteristics. Those kinds of traits are harder to manufacture than, say, what displaying a Taylor Swift CD might say about you.

SAM: I think some of the work on self-verification is relevant here. When somebody who sees themselves in a positive light wants other people to see them positively, that's no surprise. But studies have shown that people who see themselves negatively—such as people with low self-esteem—would still rather be seen negatively, because that feels more authentic. Bill Swann, who invented this theory, has done a whole series of great studies on this. In one of the studies, the subject enters a room and interacts with two people, one of whom treats them well and one who treats them badly. Then they're asked which person they would rather interact with. Those with low self-esteem would rather interact with the person who treated them badly. When people feel they're viewed authentically, the world feels more predictable to them. So they can figure out what's going on and understand how they'll be treated and how they can treat others. You see a lot of that in people's spaces, I think.

When we polish our environments before projecting them to the world, it's not about falseness, but more so about

> "Personal spaces are revealing because they crystallize many hours, weeks and months of actual living—something that's impossible to fake, unlike just an hour or two of talking to somebody."

refining the image that we identify with, so that other people can understand who we believe ourselves to be?

LINDSAY: Just because we're deliberately changing or trying to express something about ourselves doesn't mean that it's necessarily inauthentic. It's another manifestation of our personality.

How does constantly seeing other people's "more perfect" homes change the way we live in our own?

SAM: It's maybe a social context in which we know we're only seeing a subset of things. People assume that others are projecting a positive version of themselves, and given that, we discount. So when I see a photo of somebody's space on their social media feed or on an interiors blog or website, I don't think that's how it is every day. I understand that it's probably presented for that format, and I take that into account when I'm forming an impression.

LINDSAY: I totally agree. There's a certain level of intimacy you have to have with someone in order to have a conversation. It's not pleasurable to expose the negative parts of life on social media for either the audience or for the person expressing them. Many of us reserve those negative, sad things for the people we feel most connected to, but I think this is shifting. For instance, it's becoming more socially acceptable to grieve people online: both people we know and cultural icons. As people grow more accustomed to this kind of behavior, I'm curious to see what happens as we become more real with one another, and those boundaries begin to break even further.

I know several people who have obsessions with interiors websites and magazines that border on being unhealthy. Why are some people so besotted with getting a peek inside strangers' homes, even if they know they've been staged?

LINDSAY: Thinking about or seeing other people's spaces influences how we see ourselves. I've been working on a new app called Handy. We look at how people are forming impressions of others in relation to their decisions about space and social interactions. One of the things we looked at is how a person's space influences your likelihood to date them or to break up with them. We certainly make judgments about others based on their space, and it seems that we're making decisions about whether or not to continue interacting with others based on that as well.

SAM: I agree with you. Looking at people's spaces is thought to be diagnostic. If you go on a date with somebody, you can hold it together for a brief period of time. You can seem charming and pleasant and reliable for that hour if you really focus on it, but when they come to your house, it's difficult to maintain that. You can't just suddenly have a well-organized, cultured space. If you want to have tickets from some avant-garde theater performance displayed on your wall, you have to actually have gone to that avant-garde theater performance; if you want to have a highly cultural book collection that looks thumbed-through, then you have to own those books and have thumbed through them. Research shows that personal spaces are so revealing because they really crystallize many hours, weeks and months of actual living—something that's quite hard to

"As new forms of expression show up, we make use of them to express our identity. There's a lot of research showing that people are happier, healthier and more productive when others see them as they see themselves."

fake, unlike just an hour or so of talking to somebody.
LINDSAY: Exactly. Many people will "Facebook stalk" people they have just met in an effort to diagnose what that person is really like. That's what dating websites are founded on: the idea that the things that people choose to share about themselves online is diagnostic —that it's a somewhat reliable indicator of who the person is in real life.

On the flip side of this hyperawareness, people don't necessarily realize the ways they're displaying intimate areas of their lives—the open medicine cabinet in the reflection of a bathroom selfie, the tattered couch in the background of a carefully curated coffee table shot—because they're too focused on controlling what's in the foreground.
LINDSAY: Let's say I put up a picture of my living space and had it the exact way I wanted it—neat with everything in order. But Sam might look at it and say, "Oh! She's really open, because look at all of those photographs showing different locations she's got on the walls." Just because I'm deliberately trying to express one thing doesn't mean that people aren't seeing other things too: There are certain characteristics we can't control that are going to be conveyed regardless of how manufactured we make the rest of it. Communication involves so many subtle cues that it's not realistic to imagine we're communicating only one thing at a time.

Aside from the actual content, what can what we learn from the metadata surrounding social media?
SAM: Our behaviors come across in many ways—the number of posts we have, what we say in our posts, how many times we like stuff, the number of friends we have, the number of groups we're a part of and the things that are going on in our photos. Michal Kosinski at Stanford University has done research linking elements of our profiles to our personalities, such as how introverts tend to tilt their heads slightly forward in their profile pictures while extroverts have less hair on their foreheads and tend to look up. One of the reasons why social media is so informative, especially for things like extroversion, is that it shows a lot of behaviors.

What social factors are at play that have made our feelings about privacy change so swiftly? Why now?
SAM: A lot of the mental processes we see are getting played out in a world in which they didn't evolve. Much of our psychology evolved when we lived in groups of 100 to 150 people. It would be very rare to meet somebody you didn't know. There was a basic need to connect with others, maintain our social bonds, figure out what the norms are and re-establish who our allies are. That was a basic human need, and it served us very well. Then, suddenly, we had this technology to connect with not hundreds of people but with thousands of people. Our Stone Age minds have ended up in a very different world, with some funny results.

Sometimes when I walk into someone's apartment or house for the first time, I feel like I already know it and feel at home because I've seen it in the background of their feeds for so long. That makes my relationship with their

> "I think we all implicitly now understand that we tailor places to suit our own personalities and behaviors, but you now have to make your home acceptable to a broader range of people if you want to be successful."

space very different. It's not necessarily theirs—it's ours. It becomes a shared space.

LINDSAY: That's what's complicated and interesting in opening our spaces up to strangers more: It breaks down the differences and the boundaries between individuals. If we only knew each other virtually and then you came to my home after you've seen all my pictures of my cats, then you're going to potentially interact with my space in a different way—and that can be a good thing. It may make you more comfortable with me, and it may make us become friends faster. But it may also be bad, because it may lead you to overstep a boundary that you wouldn't have before. That can go either way, right? It's this complex relationship that makes me really interested in services like Airbnb: You're inviting people into your home—this space that holds all your intimate objects—and they basically have free rein without you there. It's cool because they're getting to know you, but you're not actually getting to know them. That's where that boundary breaks a little. There's a different level of intimacy—you have a different set of boundaries with me than I have with you, and that has really strong implications for the success of our social interactions down the road.

Following up on the topic of renting out our homes on Airbnb and other sub-rental markets: Compared to having friends crash on our couches for free, inviting strangers into our homes for monetary gain turns it into a business interaction. Will these services where money changes hands start to muddle our relationship with our homes?

SAM: We're required to make the public spaces of our homes more generic because we need them to be acceptable to more people. I think we all implicitly now understand that we tailor places to suit our own personalities and behaviors, but you now have to make your home acceptable to a broader range of people if you want to be successful. What would be interesting to know—and I don't know if there's been any work on it—is if the private spaces we retain for ourselves in our shared homes become more personalized as a sort of reaction to the other parts of houses that have become more generic.

LINDSAY: What might happen is that people will look for other outlets in which they can express themselves more intimately. And maybe that's part of what is happening with over-sharing on social media. That's a really big question, and I don't even know how you would empirically go about studying that! We have the need to express ourselves and connect with a space, so if we can't do that, we'll have to somehow adapt and find other outlets. One of the things I've been starting to work on is within office spaces: There's this movement toward hotel-ing and co-working and not actually having your own space to claim for yourself. And I think it's a real detriment. We've seen in past work that it's important that there's an expression of self in our spaces—it has big outcomes linked to whether or not you're going to stay at a job and feel connected with it. The same is seen within our home spaces, especially with college kids looking at whether or not they're going to stay in college based on how they're connecting to their environment. We have to have those outlets to express ourselves, and I think what will probably hap-

> "When half of a couple or one member of a family doesn't have a say over the design of a space, they'll often find some other outlet, even if it's just a basement, garage, attic or a corner of a room, any place they can call their own."

pen is that we'll adapt and shift to incorporating aspects of ourselves into other places.

There's definitely a paradox at play here: On one hand, we put so much effort into crafting these individualized spaces that accurately reflect who we are. Yet on the other, we then often dilute that highly nuanced space in order to seem more generically "likable." I tend to gravitate toward the more messy, personal-feeling ones than the ones picked straight from an IKEA catalog, for example.

SAM: Peter van der Bel in Amsterdam has been doing some very interesting work with real estate agents in helping people find new houses. Once you put in the basic parameters such as location, price and number of rooms, he does a personality test and tries to match you with the personality that previously lived in that space. And I think the same thing could apply to Airbnb. Personality is a proxy for many other things, and we know from a lot of research that you want to be around like-minded people. One of the things we do when we're looking at places—whether it's Airbnb or real estate—is to find a place that we feel matches our personality, and one shorthand way of doing that is to match our personalities with the current occupants.

One last thought: Now that we're able to turn our homes into businesses, it's taking us out of the domestic realm and into this whole new world. As the line between our domestic and professional lives starts to blur, do you think it's important that our homes hold on to being places where we can rest and feel comfortable being ourselves? Or will we adapt and find that refuge in other areas of our lives?

SAM: My suspicion is that we'll find ways to do that. One of our collaborators, Christopher Travis, has reported that often one person in a family becomes more responsible for the decor of the place. When half of a couple or one member of a family doesn't have a say over the design of a space, they'll often find some other outlet, even if it's just a basement, garage, attic or a corner of a room—any place they can call their own. That person will then often come up with reasons to go visit—"Oh, you know, I have to go work in the shed"— when really that's an excuse to just go and reconnect and spend some time in a space that's truly their own. These sorts of experiences show that we have become quite resourceful at creating these refuges. This also speaks to how important it is to have that area to ourselves—a space that's our own to meet our psychological needs and isn't overseen by someone else.

LINDSAY: I totally agree. I think that people vary in how much or how little space they need to have as that sort of personal refuge to rest and have privacy. We're actually already seeing this backlash within the workplace as we shift away from having more intimate, private offices to having open offices and more flexible spaces. But people aren't as satisfied with them, and I think that a big part of it is our lack of having a space to claim as our own. And you see that within homes too. We know that people need to have some expression of self—what's hard to determine is where that outlet is. Maybe it's on social media, maybe it's in your office, maybe it's in your car. One of the beautiful things about human evolution is that we are extraordinarily adaptive creatures, and we'll find ways of adapting to this, too.

Box by Michaël
Verheyden, staircase
model by Studio
Oliver Gustav

PHOTOGRAPHS
MIKKEL MORTENSEN

SET DESIGN
SOFIE BRÜNNER

Through a Glass Darkly

Insects have a habit of showing up when we least expect them, but from buzzes behind the curtains to cobwebs lining the cupboard, the traces they leave around our homes remind us that we've got permanent company.

Lamp by
Studio Toogood

Bowl by
PlueerSmitt
for Karakter

Candleholder by
Patricia Urquiola for
Georg Jensen

Marble circles
by Kristina Dam

Sculpture by Asger
Kristensen

WORDS
SUZANNE SNIDER

PHOTOGRAPHS
THE GLENN GOULD ESTATE

Variations

on Solitude:

Glenn

Gould

Rising to fame in the 1950s, Canadian pianist Glenn Gould catapulted classical music up the charts with his inventive, energetic interpretations of Bach and Beethoven and his antihero appeal. Retiring from the stage at the age of 33, Gould withdrew into his Toronto home and within himself. Now, three decades since his death, Gould's inner life endures with as much legend as his recordings.

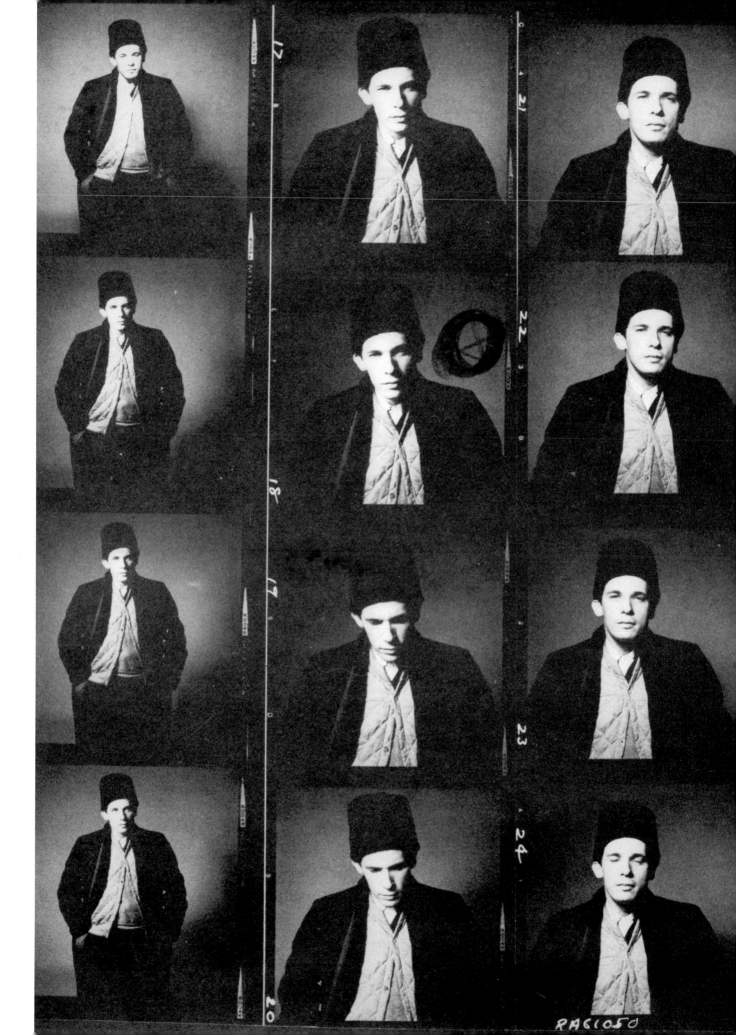

Every year, hundreds of tourists make the pilgrimage to an unexceptional art deco building known as the Park Lane Apartments in Toronto's Deer Park. They come to pay homage to the late Glenn Gould, one of the world's most famous classical pianists and composers—and a quirky and intensely private person.

Gould moved to the Park Lane Apartments in 1960 and lived there until he died in 1982 at the age of 50. Suite 902 was his first "adult" home; until age 28, the international celebrity chose to live with his parents in the Beach, a middle-class suburb of Toronto. While not architecturally significant on its own, the building—specifically his 9th-floor penthouse—was a place where Gould could fully inhabit his life as an artist without an audience.

Many regard Gould's most significant musical accomplishment to be his 1955 recording of J.S. Bach's *The Goldberg Variations*, a technically demanding piece for piano, originally written for harpsichord. The album was one of the best-selling classical albums in musical history, exciting Bach fans as well as Gould fans and converting a whole new audience to the classical music genre. In 1964, Gould decided he no longer wished to perform publicly, a position he maintained for the rest of his life. But he went on to record more than 50 albums including a second version of *The Goldberg Variations,* released shortly before he died. It was another commercial success.

Gould had superstar status in Canada, rivaling the fame of Leonard Cohen (who was born just two years after Gould in Depression-era Canada). Both artists attained international fame and refused to limit themselves to one medium. But while Cohen traveled the world, even living in several different countries, Gould remained close to home. He traveled to New York to record and perform until he announced he would stop performing and that he would move his recording operation to Toronto, largely because he hated flying on planes. At a time when most musical and literary artists left Canada, Gould's lack of wanderlust is part of the reason he was considered a national hero. And he had a unique charisma: He was an introverted antihero whose inability to compromise was seen as the ultimate in integrity. He had wide sex appeal, too, despite his litany of physical ailments and an apparent disinterest in anything other than music.

Today, a small dedication to Gould is staked in front of his Deer Park apartment building, summarizing his career. The plaque leaves out his radical radio documentaries and the depth of feeling he inspired in thousands of people who bought his albums or heard him perform: Asperger's advocates, gay men, radio enthusiasts and nationalist Canadians are some of the many groups of fans who have proudly appropriated Gould (correctly or incorrectly) as one of their own. He was the subject of a Lydia Davis short story, "Glenn Gould," and also one of the major characters in Thomas Bernhard's novel *The Loser*. He even inspired an episode of *The Simpsons*.

"I gather my inner resources from the outdoors," Gould once claimed, but he was famously mole-like in his apartment, spending most of his time indoors with dark curtains drawn and a bookcase blocking his bedroom window. According to Kevin Bazzana, a notable Gould biographer who wrote the book *Wondrous Strange,* he kept his heat set to 80 degrees Fahrenheit and the windows stayed sealed, year-round. When he did go out, he wore a wool coat, a hat, a scarf and gloves, even in summer months. To avoid germs, he occasionally tied a handkerchief over his mouth and he refused to drink tap water. When he went swimming, he insisted on wearing long rubber gloves that extended past his elbows. He complained often of feeling chilled, due to circulatory problems. For this same reason, he customarily soaked his arms in hot water for 20 minutes before each performance. And he relied on simple fare, keeping his oven and stove near-new with the help of Ritz Crackers, bouillon and Sanka. The occasional guest could expect to be offered arrowroot biscuits and instant coffee made from tap water.

Florence Gould, who first noticed her son had perfect pitch when he was three years old, was his only piano teacher until he was 10. After that, he studied at the Toronto Conservatory

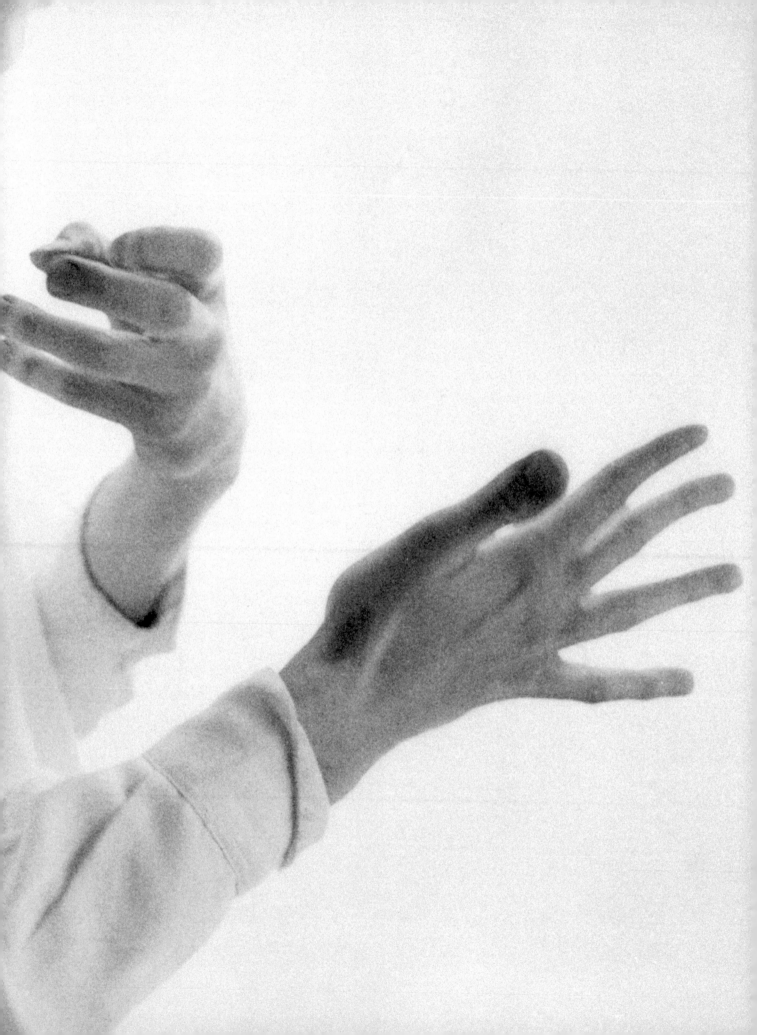

Left: Gould's favorite piano was a Chickering baby grand built in 1895, which he came across in the mid-1950s when his then-girlfriend was renting it. According to biographer Kevin Bazzana, Gould took over the rental and officially purchased the instrument in 1957. It quickly became his tactile ideal—a standard that plagued him as he encountered new pianos that failed to measure up. Throughout his career, Gould longed for the tactility of the Chickering, going so far as to perform surgery on other pianos to replicate it.

of Music with Alberto Guerrero who was most responsible for Gould's trademark finger-tapping technique. His favorite piano was a Chickering baby grand built in 1895, which became his ideal—a standard that plagued him as he encountered new pianos that failed to measure up. He noted, "It is quite unlike almost any other in the world, an extremely solicitous piano with a tactile immediacy almost like a harpsichord's." The Chickering later sat back-to-back with another baby grand in his living room. Throughout his career, he longed for the tactility of the Chickering, going so far as to perform surgery on other pianos to replicate it. One of Gould's tuners in Toronto explained, "He liked a very shallow touch... The normal key travel is about 3/8 of an inch. He wanted it about half of that, but he was always always experimenting, changing his mind, and that could happen from one day to the next."

Gould was equally particular about his seat. In 1953, his father modified a folding bridge chair for him by sawing four inches off the bottom. While typical piano benches are 20 inches off the ground, Gould's chair was only 14 inches from the ground, which gave him an entirely different physical relationship to the piano—

and terrible posture. He traveled everywhere with the chair and it sat at one of his pianos when he was home. Some photos show Gould contentedly sitting on the chair with stuffing exploding from the upholstery. When the cushion finally gave way, Gould continued to use the chair, balancing on a single wooden cross bar.

———

Apparently, he was less particular about the rest of his furniture, which was reportedly secondhand and unremarkable. Since few photographs exist, his apartment can only be reconstituted in forensic fashion, piecing it together based on those few photographs and some anecdotes. The details of Gould's living space illuminate his living strategies: how he coped, self-soothed and performed when no one was watching. When he was stuck in Israel using a piano that would not perform well for him, his remedy was to mentally transport himself back to suite 902. He explained: "...I sat in my car in the sand dune and decided to imagine myself back in my living room... and first of all to imagine the living room, which took some doing because I'd been away from it for three months at this point, and I tried to imagine where everything was in the room,

then visualize the piano, and... this sounds ridiculously yogistic, I'd never done it before in precisely these terms or anything related to it in terms of precision... but so help me it worked."

In photos, one room in the apartment looks like an archival storage area with stacks of unprocessed materials, but these piles are the result of a default position: a failure to clean, sort or discard. A photograph of this storage room shows a Grammy used as a paperweight that is half falling off the pile it anchors. His yellow legal pads, strewn throughout the apartment and found after he died, reflect Gould's sense of interior order. Most of the pads' contents are obsessive lists. He tracked various functions, maintaining lists related to the stock market, the food he ate, physical symptoms and future plans.

To his fans and many of his peers, his idiosyncrasies were evidence of genius, but his approach did not endear all of his colleagues to him. For instance, there were conductors who complained about his habit of conducting with his left hand while he played with his right. He defended that mannerism in a 1974 interview in *Rolling Stone*, asserting that such choreography is "surely a private matter between my left hand and my right,

and I cannot see why it's of concern to anybody." While most biographers have chalked up Gould's maladies to hypochondria, he is known to have suffered from excruciating back pain and high blood pressure as well as an overreliance on prescription medications. His medicine cabinet included Diazepam, Fiorinal, tetracycline and various sleeping pills prescribed by multiple doctors. In defense of his reputation, Gould insisted, "This pill complex of mine has been grossly exaggerated. Why, one reporter wrote that I traveled with a suitcase full of pills. Actually, they barely fill a briefcase."

Today, he would likely be given a diagnosis of fibromyalgia, which would explain many of his seemingly unrelated symptoms, including heightened anxiety around his health issues. He did refer to his problems with his hands as "fibrositis," a more antiquated term with which few were familiar at the time.

Gould wasn't a total shut-in, despite his reputation. He roved between several spaces that served as annexes to his apartment, including a recording studio he created at a local hotel, the CBC studios and his car. Biographer Kevin Bazzana called his car an "apartment on wheels." He especially liked to go out late at night.

Above and next spread: Despite Gould's particularity about his instrument and the folding bridge chair he used for performances, he was less picky about the furniture in his home, which was reportedly secondhand and unremarkable. Gould was an accidental preservationist as a result of hoarding, and his apartment contained piles of unprocessed archival materials, legal pads strewn across the floor and a Grammy tilted on its side, used as a makeshift paperweight.

He explained: "I don't much care for sunlight, and bright colors of any kind depress me. I schedule my errands for as late an hour as possible and I tend to emerge along with the bats and the raccoons at twilight." (From *The Life and Times of Glenn Gould*.) A frequent late-night destination was Fran's, a 24-hour diner near his apartment. He would sit in the same booth and order the same meal: eggs, side salad, Sanka, tomato juice and orange sherbet.

Close friends dispute Gould's reputation as asocial or cold. They point to his enthusiastic use of the phone to make connections—sometimes luxuriating in one- or two-hour conversations. He enjoyed the phone so much that he outfitted his car with one of the first mobile models on the market.

Even with the phone, though, he maintained control: He rarely picked up if someone called him, preferring to speak when he initiated the conversation. The description of Gould in his Park Lane apartment might sound like the moping of a failed prodigy or aimless bachelor, but one could argue that he was assiduously studying radio and TV, both of which he turned his attention to after his concert life ended. And Gould was both prolific and successful during this period. While he made disparaging comments about television

generally, he did have favorite shows: In the 1970s, he was a dedicated follower of *The Mary Tyler Moore Show*. (Gould's own *Mary Tyler Moore* dubs are now part of his archive at the National Library of Canada.) He often watched television while simultaneously listening to two different radio broadcasts. His belief that "we are capable of doing many things at once" guided his approach to life, musical composition, and later, his experimental radio documentaries.

Gould chose solitude as the subject of his first radio program, *The Idea of North*, which was broadcast by the CBC in 1967. He was attracted to perfect solitude in its extreme and saw his own compromises—watching television, for example—as weaknesses. He saw himself as a hermit, though his withdrawal from the world was imperfect. In the act of making the documentary, he expressed his reverence for the true ascetic.

Gould failed to attain that level, himself, partly because he wasn't self-sufficient. But he was insulted that he was never invited on the Canadian radio show *Hermit's Choice*. *The Idea of North* was revolutionary, adopting musical principles in its composition. Gould coined the term "contrapuntal radio" to describe this new

style. Contrapuntal radio took its lead from contrapuntal music in which independent melodies played at the same time. For *The Idea of North*, Gould interviewed five narrators about the subjects of solitude and northern Canada, weaving the voices together with ambient sound. He continued this approach with *The Latecomers* and *The Quiet in the Land*; together, these documentaries made up *The Solitude Trilogy*.

———

Glenn Gould suffered a stroke two days after his 50th birthday and died on October 4, 1982. After years of controlling his own surroundings, his final resting place—at Mount Pleasant Cemetery—is decorated weekly by tourists and local fans with items ranging from Gerbera daisies and roses to figurines and rocks. His epitaph is not set with words but with musical notes. They are fading with the passage of time, but it is fitting that they are the first three bars of *The Goldberg Variations*. While devotees still flock to the cemetery, it cannot match his apartment in terms of giving us a sense of this very private man. But it is the only place that fans can truly enter.

FURTHER READING

"Glenn Gould" from *Almost No Memory* by Lydia Davis
"The Virtuoso as Intellectual" from *On Late Style* by Edward Said
Glenn Gould: Music & Mind by Geoffrey Payzant
The Glenn Gould Reader by Tim Page
A Romance on Three Legs by Katie Hafner
Glenn Gould: A Life and Variations by Otto Friedrich
Wondrous Strange: The Life and Art of Glenn Gould by Kevin Bazzana

Left: In 1964, after performing in cities including New York, Los Angeles, Boston and Moscow, Gould retired from live performance. "Gould envisioned an idyllic retirement in which he would live alone, away from the city, writing and composing, realizing some of his bucolic ambitions," writes Bazzana in his book *Wondrous Strange*. Gould went on to record more than 50 successful albums from his home in Toronto. This included a second version of *The Goldberg Variations*, released shortly before his death in 1982. It was a rousing commercial success.

WORDS
ALEX T. ANDERSON

TABLE SETTINGS

Certain foods taste better when eaten in well-appointed settings. In this excerpt from Eating Architecture, Alex T. Anderson examines the difference between eating and dining and how the pleasures of the stomach are not only satisfied by food, but by the complex relationship between a meal, its setting and the elusive desires of its diner.

The encompassing pleasure of a good meal depends on its setting. This statement seems at first to warrant little comment. Chefs, restaurant critics and no doubt many restaurant-goers often regard it as dogma. Nevertheless, one could counter it by citing the pleasure of eating just about anywhere on an empty stomach, or the delights of takeout food, which can hardly boast an "appropriate" setting.

Of course, food can provide pleasure—to a hungry person—in virtually any context. The enjoyment associated with assuaged hunger is an unavoidable fact of our physiology, and it lies behind much of the satisfaction that dining provides. The Greek philosopher Epicurus regarded it as the basis for human artistry, contending that "the beginning and the root of all good is the pleasure of the stomach." However, the pleasure of eating differs greatly from the pleasure of dining. In the 19th century, Jean Anthelme Brillat-Savarin, one of the first and most influential writers about food, constructed the "science" of gastronomy on this presumption, declaring in *The Physiology of Taste*, "the pleasure of eating is one we share with animals... The pleasures of the table are known only to the human race."

The act of dining aspires to satisfy far more than the feral cravings of the belly. And it requires more than hunger. Brillat-Savarin reasoned that the complex, obscure and often elusive sensation of well-being that accompanies a good meal depends on painstaking preparation of the dishes, a well-chosen setting and the right combination of guests.

Contemporary chef-restaurateurs pay very close attention to these elements, and the designers of places for dining must work, using similar presumptions, to complement the production of their chefs. For the diner's part, the well-being made possible by a good and well-situated meal demands attentive ingestion of the food—and its setting—which requires an appetite.

"Sometimes the food and its setting correlate so well that the diner need do little more than participate in the spectacle presented, following where the designers of the meal lead."

One of the 20th century's great eaters, *The New Yorker's* longtime food writer A. J. Liebling, once said, "A good appetite gives an eater room to turn around in." Although he was speaking figuratively—indicating that a person who cheerfully maintains a substantial capacity to eat avails him- or herself of all the pleasure that food and a given situation might offer—the spatial image he conveys is fitting. A good appetite expands to fill out not just the body but the area surrounding it. The very human experience of dining incorporates the meal and its context.

When a meal and its setting fit particularly well, when they resonate and stir the senses, the results can be especially memorable. Often, however, this pleasure, built on the serendipitous combination of many factors, remains fleeting or elusive. Liebling calls for "good appetite" as a kind of safeguard. A good appetite improves the chances of capturing and extending moments of gustatorial pleasure. It not only gives hearty eaters room to turn around in; it also situates them well for good eating.

Sometimes the food and its setting correlate so well that the diner need do little more than participate in the spectacle presented, following where the designers of the meal lead. The Argentine storytellers Jorge Luis Borges and Adolfo Bioy Casares write of just such a trajectory in their fictional tale "An Abstract Art." In this story, they recount the invented evolution of "culinary cooking" and fabricate its obscure architectural counterpart, the tenebrarium.

The aim of culinary cooking, as they describe it, is to develop "a cuisine owing nothing to the plastic arts or to the object of nourishment," that is, a cuisine unconcerned with appearance, setting or nourishment. It seeks to satisfy only the sensation of taste. Its origins lie with the scientific discovery, in 1891, of the five fundamental tastes: sour, salty, bitter, sweet and (their addition) insipid.

Acting on this discovery, an astute Parisian chef in the story, Ishmael Querido, opens Les Cinq Saveurs, a restaurant that treats gastronomic devotees to "taste" in its most pristine state: five identical, translucent, grayish, inch-high pyramids offering each of the five tastes. Borges and Bioy Casares describe later, more complicated iterations of this cuisine that allow for the revival of "the age-old ancestral tastes," but only after all visual and tactile characteristics have been removed from the dishes that incorporate them. "Vivid colors, elegant serving platters and what common prejudice calls a well-presented dish—all these were banned."

But it is not until an audacious moment in 1932 that their fanciful history comes to its fitting conclusion, when another ingenious chef Jean-Françoise Darracq devises the proper setting for the cuisine: "[In] a restaurant like all others, serving dishes in no way different from those of the past... [he] carried out the simple act destined to place him forever at the top-most point of the pinnacle in the entire annals of cookery. He snapped out the lights. There, in that in-

stant, the first tenebrarium was launched." We are to understand from this outrageous act that, just as the great Dada artists had made context essential to their art in a single stroke (by placing a urinal, a bicycle wheel or some other ready-made object in a gallery and calling it art) so too did Darracq challenge "a handful of cognoscenti" to consider ordinary food "art" by placing it in a new setting: the darkened dining room of the tenebrarium.

In "An Abstract Art," Borges and Bioy Casares demonstrate in a roundabout, but powerful way that cuisine and setting are inextricable; a cuisine concerned only with flavor is nearly unthinkable. The diner needs the place as much as the food to experience a meal properly. The absurdly reductive "culinary cooking" and the darkened room in which one experiences it complement and require each other. Only in their fastidiously coordinated association does the anticipated pleasure unfold for the diner.

Sometimes, by contrast, a diner might discover an expansive, unexpected pleasure that unfurls itself with slight provocation from unremarkable food taken in just the right setting. Through a strange alchemy unleashed by their combination, a sense of well-being expands in the imagination, even as the specific flavors and atmosphere that precipitated it fade.

Marcel Proust recounts such an event, in a well-known passage of *Remembrance of Things Past*, when on a cheerless afternoon in Combray his mother offers him tea and

"Just as gastronomic pleasure encompasses more than satisfaction of hunger, so too does it include more than the meal and its distractions. Gastronomic pleasure involves the intellect."

a petite madeleine: "And soon, mechanically, dispirited after a dreary day with the prospect of a depressing morrow, I raised to my lips a spoonful of the tea in which I had soaked a morsel of the cake. No sooner had the warm liquid mixed with the crumbs touched my palate than a shudder ran through me and I stopped, intent upon the extraordinary thing that was happening to me. An exquisite pleasure had invaded my senses, something isolated, detached, with no suggestion of its origin."

Seeking to prolong this pleasure and to find its source, Proust takes a second and a third mouthful, but begins to lose the sensation. To force it back to consciousness, he says, "I shut out every obstacle, every extraneous idea, I stop my ears and inhibit all attention against the sounds from the next room... I clear an empty space in front of it." And at last winning back the sensation of pleasure again, Proust finds that far from existing in an empty space, it has attached itself to a place that takes shape and grows in his consciousness.

"And as soon as I had recognised the taste of the piece of madeleine soaked in her decoction of lime-blossom which my aunt used to give me...the old grey house upon the street, where her room was, rose up like a stage set...and with the house the town...the streets along which I used to run errands, the country roads we took when it was fine."

It is not the immediate sensation of taste or of satiated hunger that interests Proust, but the rich, pleasurable evocation

that the aroma and flavor of tea and taste of the madeleine bring about. From them he raises up the room, the house and the village—with all of their characteristic odors, colors, textures.

Liebling lamented, in a memoir of his first years of serious eating, *Between Meals*, that "in the light of what Proust wrote with so mild a stimulus, it is the world's loss that he did not have a heartier appetite." What Proust might have conjured one can hardly imagine. Nevertheless, the frugality of the event serves to demonstrate how manifold and expansive the relationship between food and its setting can become.

A good appetite helps one capture and make sense of far more complex experiences, but it also has limits. Gourmands, even those with the most impressive capacities, have deplored the constraints of appetite since before the fabled days of Roman vomitoria. Brillat-Savarin suggests that the science and art of gastronomy developed as an antidote to these limits; in "Meditation 14" of the *Physiology of Taste* he writes, "poets long ago began to complain that the throat, being too short, limited the length of the pleasure of tasting."

To advance beyond the pleasure of taste, beyond the confines of the alimentary passages and into the dining room, gastronomy enlisted the help of other arts. For the most sumptuous meals, the ancients contributed music and entertainments of all sorts. They filled the air with perfumes and placed ornaments on anything that could support them. The French maîtres

d'hôtel in the courts of Louis XIV and XV sought to surpass the ancients. These masters of fantastic baroque feasts added elaborate artificial dinner "sets" arranged in monumentally reconfigured gardens and surmounted by profusions of fountains and pompous displays of fireworks. Such "artificial embellishments" aim to arouse every sense. The attention of ears, nose, hands and eyes is drawn toward these, even as the mouth and stomach ingest a great succession of lavish dishes.

Just as gastronomic pleasure encompasses more than satisfaction of hunger, so too does it include more than the meal and its distractions. Gastronomic pleasure also involves the intellect. A good meal piques the imagination, conjures memories, conveys ideas. Often, it does so through surprising combinations, placing flavors in resonance with each other and with their settings to provoke the complacent and astonish the alert diner. To discover this kind of pleasure demands not only appetite but also attention.

Adventurous diners often seek such pleasure in the variety that a change of venue provides—by going to many different restaurants, for example, or by traveling to "exotic" places. Italo Calvino vividly demonstrates the benefits of the latter in "Under the Jaguar Sun," a fictional essay on taste. Its Italian protagonists, the narrator and his wife, Olivia, approaching middle age, undertake a gustatorial journey in Mexico. Through a series of shared encounters with the artifacts of the culture, intensified by its characteristic and idiosyncratic cuisine, they discover fascinating shades of a Mexico that would otherwise have remained obscure to them.

At first, they take exquisite, mutual delight in the food, but a dawning awareness of the places that surround them augments this gratification. A deeply satisfying comprehension of their surroundings—and its sometimes sordid past—emboldens their pleasure in the food.

In one instance, as they savor piquant dishes under the orange trees of an old convent, they sense the latent passions of aristocratic nuns subdued long ago in the dark rooms that surround them. In their quiet confinement, these nuns had created audacious, complex, unsettling meals not merely to exercise their considerable culinary abilities, nor solely "to satisfy the venial whims of gluttony."

Their recipes also expressed the ardor of more consequential fantasies, carnal fantasies: "the fantasies, after all, of sophisticated women...whose reading told of ecstasies and transfigurations, martyrs and tortures." As they taste these exquisite dishes, Olivia and her husband recognize the same clandestine passions they had earlier discovered enfolded into the ornate baroque churches of Oaxaca:

"Architecture...the background to the lives of those religious; it, too, was impelled by the same drive toward the extreme that led to the exacerbation of flavors amplified by the blaze of the most spicy chiles. Just as colonial baroque set no limits on the profusion of ornament and display, in which God's presence was identified in a closely calculated delirium of brimming, excessive sensations, so the curing of the hundred or more native varieties of hot peppers carefully selected for each dish opened vistas of flaming ecstasy."

Thus, the apparently unremarkable scene that Calvino places before the reader—of a tourist couple enjoying a meal together in a cloister garden—becomes a passionate exploration of an unfamiliar place. Its subtleties reveal themselves only as flavors resonate with the intricacies of its buildings and landscapes—the somber, cracked plaster walls, the incomprehensible scrollwork and gilded ceilings, the jungle-shrouded ruins, the shimmering sunlight, the aroma of orange blossoms.

These harmonies reveal another important aspect of the pleasure derived from the settings for cuisine: It often reaches well beyond the dining room and into its regional context. Terrain, habits and legend often manifest themselves in the cuisine of a place. They appear in the recipes that incorporate local ingredients, in the special tools and methods used for their preparation and in the environments most suitable for their consumption.

Accordingly, the cuisine of Oaxaca that Calvino describes developed characteristic "embellishments" that exploit local ingredients, recall native histories and embody indigenous values. Similarly, the cuisines of the Dordogne in France, of Hunan in China and of Northern California in the US distinguish themselves largely through the unique appurtenances—architecture, furniture, tools and ingredients—with which they developed over time.

A "foreign" visitor to such a place may even sense that the central idea behind a meal there is its regional identity. This is certainly true in the dining room of Chez Panisse, Alice Waters' restaurant in Northern California. Its verdant entry terrace modulates the strong California sunshine, the oil-rubbed woodwork and furniture recall the arts and crafts tradition of the West Coast, and the food, Waters says, is a "celebration of the very finest of our regional food products."

Transplanted into another environment—into an "exotic" restaurant somewhere in an American city, or into a takeout box—the characteristic embellishments of a particular cuisine fall out of place. In many cases, regional context is as essential to the experience of a good meal as the dining room, table or plates set before the diner.

If, as Epicurus tells us, the pleasure of the stomach is the beginning of all good, then a well-situated meal shows us that, for the attentive diner with an excellent appetite, the pleasure of eating extends outward to incorporate the immediate dining environment and place setting.

An extended version of this essay appears in the book Eating Architecture *edited by Jamie Horwitz and Paulette Singley (MIT Press, 2004).*

WORDS
TRISTAN RUTHERFORD

PHOTOGRAPHS
KRISTOFER JOHNSSON

Lover's Discourse: Villa Santo Sospir

A visitor who arrives for dinner, paints the walls and stays for 11 years is unlikely to receive another warm welcome—unless that visitor is artist Jean Cocteau. Once host to Picasso, Marlene Dietrich and Greta Garbo, Villa Santo Sospir now stands as a living monument to the Dionysian excess of 1950s France.

If only the walls could talk. Fortunately, at the Villa Santo Sospir they actually can. In 1950, painter, filmmaker and bohemian all-rounder Jean Cocteau came for dinner. He ended up staying 11 years. The white walls of the newly built villa weren't to his taste, so he proceeded to fresco nude Greek mythological dreamscapes above the fireplace. Over the next decade Cocteau simply carried on "tattooing" (to use his term) the entire edifice. More fortunately still, the villa's owner didn't mind.

That's because Cocteau's host was Francine Weisweiller. An extraordinarily well-connected Parisian socialite, she was among the first patrons of Yves Saint Laurent, and artists like Raoul Dufy and designers like Cristóbal Balenciaga attended her regular salons. Coco Chanel was a pal. It

was the age when artists and aristocrats of any persuasion could drop in at the Villa Santo Sospir to shoot movies, daub canvases, wine and dine. And so they did. The mansion at the end of Cap Ferrat, a sun-licked peninsula on the Côte d'Azur, was simply the perfect place to party.

Amazingly, that carefree post-war epoch has been preserved in situ. Visitors today will find casual snapshots of Pablo Picasso wedged above the mantelpiece. Notes written by Cocteau in the 1950s tacked up beside his bedroom mirror. An invitation to attend an exhibition in the company of President Charles de Gaulle tucked into a bookshelf. It's like Cocteau and Weisweiller were discussing Picasso's latest muse over a bottle of Pouilly-Fuissé—then just up and left.

The property's guide and caretaker is Eric Marteau. He's a genial host who worked as Weisweiller's nurse beginning in 1982, becoming a trusted friend to both Francine and her daughter, Carole, the villa's current owner. "It's a living museum," says Marteau. "There are few like it in the world." The walls of the main salon are so densely decorated it's like gorging on a private Cocteau gallery. Bamboo loungers invite guests to flop down—where Picasso and his lover Jacqueline Roque would have—and gaze across the room. Marlene Dietrich and Greta Garbo once ate at the salon's dining table. Both guests broke the carefree code that still suffuses the Villa Santo Sospir by chatting only to Cocteau (Marlene Dietrich) and refusing to say a word (Greta Garbo).

Eric's tour leads to the bedrooms on the villa's lower story. The staircase down is playful: A life-size drawing of a sleeping angel glides above the walkway. The steps are carpeted in leopard print. "The villa decor was styled by Madeleine Castaing," the doyenne of interior designers who introduced the animal print into elegant society, explains Eric. At the bottom of the stairs, a giant dislocated finger points to the word "DORMIR" and a discreet artist's signature reads "Jean, 1950."

Carole Weisweiller's bedroom is first up. She was eight years old when, on the wall opposite her bed, Cocteau drew a vast mural of Dionysus, the god of wine, sleeping

off a party. As a testament to the artist's place as an intimate invitee, he slept in the bedroom next door.

Like every other room in the house, Cocteau's bedroom is a time capsule of paraphernalia from six decades ago. Tacked on the wall is a fading postcard of Cocteau's portrait by Modigliani (he was also painted by Raoul Dufy and photographed by Man Ray). A letter alongside could have been jotted yesterday, but was in fact written in 1958. The principal fresco here witnesses the Greek god Pan feeding bread to two unicorns. "The unicorn's horns form a pyramid—a Freemason symbol—while the bread represents the Cor-

pus Christi," explains Eric. The motif sums up the mythological, spiritual and religious medley that preoccupied Cocteau's work. "And because Pan loved both men and women, the character was a gay symbol in the 19th and 20th centuries."

Cocteau was perfectly open about his own sexuality. The bedroom of his lover, the impossibly handsome Édouard Dermit, shares the simple bathroom next door. Dermit, who Cocteau affectionately called "Doudou" and who became his adoptive son—therefore his sole heir—was decorated with a Narcissus and Echo painting across all four walls. As Carole Weisweiller once told *The New York Times*: "Cocteau

> "Cocteau liked to say that he learned from Matisse that once you paint one wall, the other three look bare."
>
> CAROLE WEISWEILLER

"She was eight years old when, on the wall opposite her bed, Cocteau drew a vast mural of Dionysus, the god of wine, sleeping off a party."

liked to say that he learned from Matisse that once you paint one wall, the other three look bare." On Dermit's bookshelf sits an ancient tourist guide to Madrid's Museo del Prado, plus some comic books—a graphic novel combination of which inveterate wordsmith and doodler Cocteau no doubt approved.

A second set of stairs leads back to the airy main salon. This capacious space is like a breath of air after the art-filled cacophony downstairs. From the salon, the Villa Santo Sospir's garden terrace tumbles to the sea. Butterflies bumble around bougainvillea. Cap Ferrat's famous parakeets cheep-cheep near the water, each green bird the offspring of a local dilettante's

abandoned menagerie. Cocteau the auteur shot avant-garde movies in these subtropical grounds. These include *La Villa Santo Sospir*, a 35-minute montage filmed in 1952 that guides viewers around the Weisweiller home. (Spoiler alert: The villa looks exactly the same then as it does today.) The terrace view also sweeps a mile across the Mediterranean to Villefranche, where Cocteau had previously lived at the Welcome Hotel. In Villefranche, he frescoed yet another masterpiece, the interior of the Chapel of St. Pierre (also open to the public), with more muscle-bound Greek dramas. When he slacked off from his prodigious work habit he would row his friend Picasso back across to Cap Ferrat.

Back inside the villa there are countless portraits of the polymath, ever dandified in a suit and tie. There is Cocteau in Oxford, where he received an honorary doctorate in 1956. Plus Cocteau in Cannes, where he served as president of the Film Festival in 1953. But the artwork that best sums up his 1950s existence is another wall mural of Pan. The playful god is holding a local *fougasse* loaf above two tasty sea urchins, of the kind plucked from the warm waters below the villa.

Such simple sun-kissed pleasures are what this charmed house is all about. "It was like death to be taken too seriously," Cocteau once said. The walls of the Villa Santo Sospir certainly agree.

WORDS
ANDREA CODRINGTON LIPPKE

ILLUSTRATIONS
CHIDY WAYNE

Memento Mori

Family heirlooms are bequeathed when we die, but what happens to the other things we leave behind? Andrea Codrington Lippke examines the ways in which our most ordinary household objects continue their lives after we're gone.

There is an unsettling time after the death of a loved one during which inanimate possessions become unmistakably alive—more alive, in fact, than the person to whom they once belonged. I experienced this last October when, over a 10-day period of home hospice care, my mother went from being a familiar, though very ill, presence, to an entirely alien absence.

A week later, I was expecting a rush of emotions when I sorted through those possessions that were most emblematic of her and was confused by the fact that I felt practically nothing as I made piles to throw away, give away or keep myself. What I wasn't prepared for was my reaction to the random array of everyday objects that populated her side of the bathroom vanity.

Ultimately, it was a hairbrush that triggered my grief—relegated to the darkest recesses of my mother's cabinet but still bearing strands of her fine blonde hair. I put it in a small makeup bag and packed it along with her favorite books, art supplies, pieces of jewelry and clothing and brought it home with me, wondering at the seeming irrationality of the action. If I had been living during Victorian times, perhaps I would have incorporated my mother's hair into mourning jewelry—a ring that bore a small image painted by individual strands or a bracelet formed out of braided locks. Instead, eight months later and long after my mother's other belongings have been integrated into my household, the hairbrush still sits in its small bag in the corner of my bedroom, unused and untouched. I know I will never throw it away but also can't bring myself to look at it—and I don't really understand why.

Maybe my first mistake is in thinking that objects are just things—industrial helpmates, as in the case of my mother's hairbrush, whose only meaning is derived from the service they provide. Hannah Arendt, the 20th-century philosopher, expressed a much higher opinion of the nature of "the things of the world," which she believed had the function of "stabilizing human life" in the flow of time. "Men," she writes in her 1958 book

The Human Condition, "their ever-changing nature notwithstanding, can retrieve their sameness, that is their identity, by being related to the same chair and the same table."

If Arendt is right and we do gain our identity in part by interacting with the world of objects, then could it be that the inverse is also true? Material culture theorists, like the University of Southern California anthropologist Janet Hoskins, advocate for the existence of "biographical objects" that take on attributes of the people who own them. While Hoskins' studies revolve around fieldwork she undertook on an Indonesian island, there are others—like the renowned psychologist Mihaly Csikszentmihalyi—who have extended the idea to the average Western household. "When someone invests psychic energy in an object," he writes in The Meaning of Things: Domestic Symbols and the Self, "that object becomes 'charged' with the energy of the agent." He illustrates the point with the example of his favorite armchair and how the act of sitting in its well-worn velvet embrace has shaped his consciousness to such an extent that the "chair is as much a part of myself as anything can possibly be."

More than mere objects then, the things that populate our lives—armchairs, yes, but also hairbrushes—contain our very presence. And that, of course, is what becomes so upsetting when someone dies and their possessions suddenly become stand-ins.

Los Angeles–based photographer Catherine Opie experienced this when, in 2011, she spent six months shooting the contents of Elizabeth Taylor's house as an indirect portrait of the film star. Despite such unprecedented proximity to Taylor's belongings, Opie never actually met the Hollywood icon. The resulting series, 700 Nimes Road, captures the expected trappings of the actress's public life— the jewelry, shoes, gowns and celebrity photos—side by side with traces of a more quotidian existence: a jumble of emery boards in a kitschy porcelain cup, a dog-eared instruction manual for a remote control, scrape marks on the kitchen wall made by a red chair.

Halfway through Opie's project, Taylor unexpectedly died, leaving the artist to photograph the house as it was being dismantled. All of a sudden Opie was making a post-mortem portrait. Though

the majority of the 3,000 photos she took were straightforward documentary images, Opie chose to shoot Taylor's jewelry after her death with an uncharacteristically soft focus—an effort to place them "as memory, moving light," as she says in an article in The Guardian.

Though 700 Nimes Road does provide a moving and unexpectedly human portrait of Taylor, looking through the images with an eye to spotting the traces of a real life lived feels somehow transgressive. In her 1969 book Biographical Objects, French sociologist Violette Morin writes that "to meddle in the space between a biographical object and its owner is always…the act of a voyeur." But how do we deal with things that have been orphaned by the deceased except by meddling? And how do we meddle with these things without feeling at the very least terrible—and sometimes even terrified?

Literature is filled with instances of melancholy encounters with objects that have been left behind. In her autobiographical book A Very Easy Death, Simone de Beauvoir relays the experience of coming upon her dead mother's knitting basket and feeling an emotion that "rose

up and drowned us." She goes on to write that "Everyone knows the power of things: life solidified in them, more immediately present than in any one of its instants." Paul Auster's *The Invention of Solitude* intensifies the emotional heat even more. "There is nothing more terrible," he writes, "than having to face the objects of a dead man… they say something to us standing there not as objects but as remnants of thought, of consciousness." Even Joan Didion, the ultimate exemplar of literary sangfroid, describes her experience of coming across her late husband's things in fraught terms. "When I walked into the apartment and saw John's jacket and scarf still lying on the chair," she writes in *The Year of Magical Thinking,* "I wondered what an uncool customer would be allowed to do. Break down? Require sedation? Scream?"

What to do, then, with these rogue reminders of loved ones that, at least in the short term, bring more pain than pleasure? The obvious answer is to get rid of them, although this can bring up further emotional complications. A Harlem-based performance artist named Nate Hill hit upon an idea in 2009 that provided one solution. Clad in all black clothes and an oversized plastic bear head, Hill offered heartsick New Yorkers the services of Death Bear, a character who, according to his website, "will take things from you that trigger painful memories and stow them away in his cave where they will remain forever allowing you to move on with your life."

Usually the people who called upon Death Bear were suffering from a recent breakup—"women with love letters or guys with underwear," Hill explains—but in one instance he was contacted by someone who insisted on meeting in a Brooklyn park rather than at home. "The man came up," he remembers, "and handed me an eyeglass case. Inside it was a bullet, a picture of a female soldier and dog tags." Though the man revealed nothing about the origin of the objects, they were enough for Hill to form a narrative that was affecting even to him—a total stranger. "I broke down inside the mask after he turned away to go," he admits.

Orphan objects are by nature unsettling for the very reason that they have lost their fixed identity. "Death makes all material possessions nomadic," writes sociologist Margaret Gibson in *Objects of the Dead: Mourning and Memory in Everyday Life.*

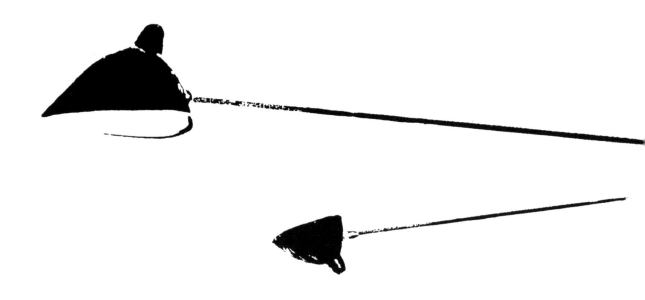

On top of being reminders of the person who has died, their in-between status can serve to destabilize our own sense of solidity in the world, becoming unwitting memento mori in the process.

The Brooklyn-based documentary photographer Jennifer Loeber discovered this for herself in 2013 after sorting through her recently deceased mother's belongings. She gathered several bags' worth of things—including clothing, boots and the contents of a makeup pouch—but ended up storing them for months in the back of a closet because they were too painful to deal with. "Knowing that those bags of her things were in my closet serving no real purpose other than upsetting me every time I reached for clean towels began to eat away at me," she remembers.

Loeber hit upon an idea while organizing family photos and noticing that many of the images showed her mother interacting with the things she had instinctively chosen to keep. "I began pairing objects with images and playing around with the connections between the two," she says. Rather than set up a studio shoot, which seemed overwhelming to the grieving photographer, Loeber took iPhone photos and started

posting the images to Instagram. The result was not only the beginnings of a poignant series called "Left Behind," but a grounding amidst the swirling aftermath of death. "The simplified approach to photographing the images took the sting out of the process and allowed me to just be in the moment," she says. Sometimes the relationship between object and photo is direct—a pearl ring that appears in a vintage image of her mother holding a white parakeet, for instance—but often the pairing is more associative and all the more resonant for it. Loeber's most affecting image features the matching of a well-worn tube of Revlon lipstick and a photo of her as a young girl in her mother's arms. Rather than remain an aching reminder of very personal absence, the lipstick has been transmuted into an artwork that has universal meaning.

Of course, there have been civilizations in times past that believed the best place for a person's belongings was in the afterlife itself. Although most early ancient Egyptians were interred in sandpits, archaeologist Howard Carter's 1922 discovery of the tomb of Tutankhamun shed light on later ornate burial practices. The tomb prominently featured more than 5,000 objects—many of

which were so-called "grave goods" meant to aid the deceased pharaoh in navigating the spirit world in style. Vikings were also often buried with objects that were thought to be of use in the afterlife—or at the very least represent their worldly value to the underworld. The most impressive Norse grave goods discovery, the Oseberg Viking ship, was unearthed in Norway in 1904 and included an ornately decorated oak vessel containing beds, carts, sleighs, chests, buckets, textiles, tools and seven wild apples—sustenance, no doubt, for the two women buried along with it.

Though it may be easy to pawn off the idea of grave goods as too literal and a thing of the past, John Troyer, director of the Centre for Death & Society at the University of Bath in the UK, points out that this isn't the case. "If you talk to any funeral director," he says, "you'll find that people are always putting stuff in coffins." If 19th- and 20th-century archaeologists were able to piece together former civilizations through the discovery of ancient grave goods, then it's potentially disturbing to think of what future academics will make of us. Amy Cunningham, a Brooklyn-based "death educator" and funeral director, says

that in her many years of work in the field she has only encountered a few instances of contemporary grave goods—once when mourners left a baseball cap and some beer in a coffin and another time when the friends of a deceased 13-year-old left him with his favorite sandwich.

There are other cultures that abstract the concept of grave goods by trading in actual objects for symbolic ones. In an elaborate version of traditional joss— the ritual immolation of paper money to ensure that the deceased prosper in the hereafter—some contemporary Chinese mourners burn bamboo paper sculptures of everything their family member used in life, or wanted to. A series of images by the Hong Kong–based artist Kurt Tong called "In Case it Rains in Heaven" shows the ways in which consumerism has impacted this sacrosanct tradition.

A video that accompanies the photographs shows the burning of everything from household tools like rice cookers, microwaves, electric fans and hairdryers to status symbols like Louis Vuitton bags, iPhones, BMWs—even a Kalashnikov automatic rifle. In one bizarre instance of artifice meeting life, a merchant

of such funeral supplies in New York's Chinatown was arrested for copyright infringement in 2011. The offending items: a paper handbag that sported a fake Burberry logo and one that bore the telltale Louis Vuitton insignia.

Carpenters in Accra, Ghana, have created a thriving industry for "fantasy" coffins that resemble a tool of the deceased's trade or an object of passion, daily use or desire. The trend evolved from the tradition of burying chieftains on the palanquins that carried them during their lifetime. Why not, midcentury craftsmen wondered, also create funerary vessels that related to the life of commoners? The first such object, according to Ga ethnic history, was designed by a carpenter named Seth Kane Kwei, who in the mid-1950s sent his grandmother into the afterlife in a coffin shaped like the airplanes she admired at the recently built Kotoka International Airport. More than half a century later, Accra is filled with artisans creating elaborate fantasy coffins—everything from hammers, pens and cameras to Nike Air sneakers, Mercedes sedans and Nokia cell phones. A recent feature by British filmmaker Benjamin Wigley called *Paa Joe & The Lion*

"In the end, maybe it's exactly those humble, uncurated objects that form the real stories of our lives."

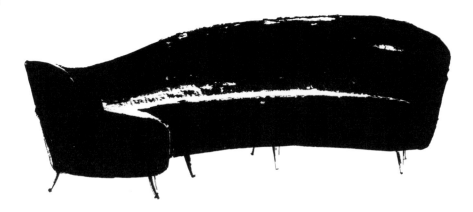

premiered at the Sheffield Documentary Festival this June, exploring the life and times of one of Ghana's most renowned coffin craftsmen, whose work has been collected by the British Museum, the Smithsonian and the Brooklyn Museum.

While consumer brand names may continue endowing the dead with status in China and Ghana, in the US sometimes it is the anonymous objects of deceased celebrities that pass on a special aura to the living. When Sotheby's auctioned off the belongings of Jackie Kennedy Onassis in 1996, even the estate's most unspectacular objects brought in outsized bids—including a lot comprised of old magazines for $12,650, a monogrammed tape measure for $45,000 and a collection of three pillows for $25,300. "They are on their way now," snarked *Newsweek* writer Jerry Adler, "crated and nestled in bubble wrap or tucked in Louis Vuitton carry-ons, carrying their little spark of cachet to Grosse Pointe, River Oaks or Malibu and many other places Jackie wouldn't have been caught dead in."

Despite an estimated intrinsic worth of $4.6 million, Jackie's estate gained a whopping $34.5 million on the sales, mostly on the merit of celebrity provenance.

In an age when everyone can have his or her proverbial 15 minutes of fame, it seems fitting that even the detritus of celebrity can become priceless. In arguably one of his most cunning moves, Andy Warhol realized that the ephemera of his life would one day prove valuable so began collecting it in boxes that were sealed and stowed as makeshift time capsules.

Flyers, postage stamps, greeting cards and knick-knacks exist side by side with such unlikely keepsakes as toenail clippings, rotting food and dead ants—a seemingly haphazard assemblage of items that was nonetheless curated by the artist. The Andy Warhol Museum in Pittsburgh is the repository of all 612 boxes, which have been carefully opened and meticulously archived and bear a Tutankhamun-like trove of insight for art historians and Warhol fans.

When hundreds of people lined up at the museum for a chance to view contents culled from Warhol's penultimate time capsule, BBC radio presenter Lenny Henry described the event in funerary terms—"like people walking past an open coffin," though instead of a body there were the material remains of his life. Warhol the person (as opposed to persona) was famously afraid

of death—obsessed, even, as evidenced in many series that involved imagery such as car crashes, electric chairs, suicides, skulls and last suppers. More revealing, perhaps, than his cannily curated capsules is a photograph taken of the artist's studio shortly after his death in 1987.

Amidst a welter of boxes, shopping bags, a sculpture of Hercules and no fewer than three pieces of exercise equipment sits a sculptural representation of Leonardo da Vinci's *Last Supper* as well as one of the massive canvases that Warhol painted on the famous religious theme.

Life and death, the sacred and profane, heroism and humility: These are the themes that emerge from Warhol's distinctly unmediated studio space—and ones that are perhaps more telling than any time capsule could be.

In the end, maybe it's exactly those humble, uncurated objects that form the real stories of our lives—my mother's orphaned hairbrush included. And while objects may be a poor stand-in for a person, they do provide what the English poet David Whyte in "Everything is Waiting for You" calls "the grand array; the swelling presence, and the chorus, crowding out your solo voice."

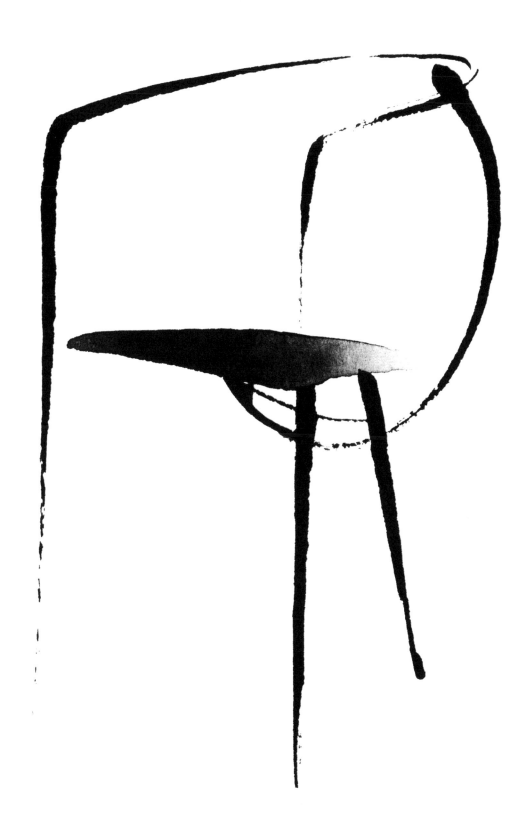

WORDS
CHARLES MOORE

PHOTOGRAPHS
NEIL BEDFORD

STYLING
CAROLYNE RAPP

In Praise of Shadows

Japanese novelist Jun'ichiro Tanizaki's essay In Praise of Shadows filters ordinary pleasures through a tranquil half-light, illuminating how light and shade's dependence on one another nuances everyday moments with repose and beauty.

First published in 1933, *In Praise of Shadows* shines a light on Japanese aesthetics and how, when light falls upon spaces and objects, grace is cast in its shade. For American educator and architect Charles Moore, reading Tanizaki's delicate prose came "with the thrill of a slap." Here, Moore's introduction to an English translation, written during a post at the UCLA School of Architecture, discusses the charm in realizing the unseen.

"One of the basic human requirements is the need to dwell, and one of the central human acts is the act of inhabiting, of connecting ourselves, however temporarily, with a place on the planet which belongs to us and to which we belong. This is not, especially in the tumultuous present, an easy act (as is attested by the uninhabited and uninhabitable no-places in cities everywhere), and it requires help: We need allies in inhabitation.

Fortunately, we have at hand many allies, if only we call on them; other upright objects, from towers to chimneys to columns, stand in for us in sympathetic imitation of our own upright stance. Flowers and gardens serve as testimonials to our own care, and breezes loosely captured can connect us with the very edge of the infinite. But in the West our most powerful ally is light. 'The sun never knew how wonderful it was,' the architect Louis Kahn said, 'until it fell on the wall of a building.' And for us the act of inhabitation is mostly performed in cahoots with the sun, our staunchest ally, bathing our world or flickering through it, helping give it light.

It comes with the thrill of a slap for us then to hear praise of shadows and darkness; so it is when there comes to us the excitement of realizing that musicians everywhere make their sounds to capture silence or that architects develop complex shapes just to envelop empty space. Thus darkness illuminates for us a culture very different from our own; but at the same time it helps us to look deep into ourselves to our own inhabitation of the world, as it describes with spine-tingling insights the traditional Japanese inhabitation of theirs. It could change our lives."

Previous spread: He
wears a turtleneck and
blazer by Issey Miyake
Left: He wears a turtle-
neck by Damir Doma,
cardigan by CMMN
SWDN and trousers by
Margaret Howell
Above: He wears a top
by Mathew Miller, car-
digan by CMMN SWDN
and jacket by Marni

This page: He wears a
sweater by Marni and
blazer by Joseph
Right: He wears a shirt
by Lemaire, sweater by
A.P.C., blazer by Hermès,
trousers by Marni and
shoes by Grenson. Beo-
Vision Horizon television
from Bang & Olufsen

He wears a top and neck piece by Lacoste, jacket by Nanamica, trousers by Paul Smith and shoes by Grenson

Left: He wears
a shirt by Dior Homme
and sweater by Joseph
This page: He wears
a shirt by Hermès,
sweater by Margaret
Howell and blazer by
Calvin Klein

INTERVIEW
RACHEL EVA LIM

PHOTOGRAPHS
ANDERS SCHØNNEMANN

A Day in the Life: T-Michael

Known for his meticulous attention to detail and for his garments' impeccable construction, bespoke tailor T-Michael derives as much satisfaction from the design process as he does from the end result.

From the crowded cobblestone streets of London to the quiet alleyways of Bergen, Norway, T-Michael creates hand-sewn menswear that may as well come with its own lovingly worn-in passport. Born and raised as the youngest of five children in Accra, Ghana, Michael Tetteh Nartey moved to London as a teenager before traversing the North Sea to Norway at the age of 23. After earning a degree in men's tailoring, he launched his eponymous line in 1996 and now also collaborates with Alexander Helle on Norwegian Rain, a collection of hardy and sartorial rainwear with a Japanese approach. Though his work often keeps him busy, he makes time for a quiet breather on his couch or a spot of whiskey at one of his favorite neighborhood bars.

What was your first experience as a tailor and how did you get into the profession of tailoring? — When I moved to Bergen with my then-wife, the job opportunities weren't great, and that forced me to rethink everything I'd done and choose a path that'd make me and my family feel comfortable. I decided to get into clothing and jumped right into it. It may not have been the most sensible choice, but it felt like the right thing to do at the time. When I graduated from my tailoring course, I opened up my first store on a street in the city that most people don't frequent: It was a slow street, but the upside was that when people walked along it they slowed down and didn't have a sense of urgency about themselves—I thought that might just get them inside. But then I got fed up with waiting for people to come and order navy blue two-button suits, so I decided to start my own collection. I stitched the pieces in the back room, put them on a dummy and displayed them in the window.

What advice do you have for someone undergoing a career change? — It's a cliché to say, "Follow your heart," because your heart doesn't pay the bills, but things are going to get tough either way. And it's much easier to keep going if you're actually doing something you really have a passion for. It means you can stay up all night and work 24 hours

a day, because it feels right. Of course you need to get your skills in order, but choose what you *truly* want to be working with.

How does your training as a tailor separate you from other clothing designers? — I think it's made all the difference. I like to say that I design and build things up—I don't just sketch and produce them. I know how to pattern cut, I know how to trim, I know how to fit and I know how to stitch. I understand the DNA of clothing. I used to go to secondhand stores and buy tailored jackets and suits just so I could rip them apart to see how they were built up. The reason why they'd been preserved all those years is because they were built well—garments that are built well mold better on the body and get better with age. You might not like my designs, but when you wear them the fit is *bang on.* I think that's what sets me apart from other designers that may not have a tailoring background.

How is the world of tailoring going to change with the next generation? — I was part of the last batch of pure tailoring students to study at the school I attended in Bergen. After that it revised its program to blend tailoring with design. The problem with how tailoring and design are taught today is that there isn't enough emphasis on spending time getting to know the craft: People want to create things because they want to be known, not because they truly want to build something.

Why is it important for you to focus on getting the little details just right? — I think I do it more for myself than for my customers. Sometimes I put details in my garments that people will either probably not notice or won't really take the time to figure out, but for me, those tiny details are what make the garment. For example, I could make a suit and take away all the pinstripes except for a single one that runs down the left sleeve. To me, that's absolutely beautiful. It changes everything. It goes from being a simple, classic gray suit to being something different. That's what finishes a product.

What was your experience of growing up in Ghana? — I was my parents' last kid, so by the time I came along they had already tried every way of parenting and were sort of like, "Whatever, mate!" But it was brilliant having four older siblings to look up to. I don't go back to Ghana very often, but when I do, I get that feeling of being home and being back where I grew up—it's the vibrancy of being a Ghanaian. Sometimes that disappears when you live as far away as Norway, but it only takes a few hours of being in Ghana before it flashes back.

What parts of your childhood have had the biggest influence on your work? — I reckon the small things you see and experience growing up really make an impact. My dad was always well turned-out: He used to constantly polish his shoes, and I personally never want my shoes to be dirty because of that. Little things like that stay with you and form you in the later years.

Do people have many preconceived ideas about Ghanian culture? — Many people expect my designs to have bold, loud colors or patterns because that's what's *supposed* to be Ghanaian or African. And I beg to differ. Sure, we have certain parts of our culture that are bold and bright, but we have loads of other things as well. People like to ask me, "What's Ghanaian or African in your collection?" And I tell them, "Well, that's the baseline." It's where everything stems from. Everything I do is Ghanaian—it resonates deep inside of me and dictates all that I do. Ghanaians have a certain sense of subtlety and humbleness, and we have a deep sense of respect for the elderly in our society. I see a lot of similarities when I go to Japan. This attitude or sentiment just sort of lies there—you don't talk about it, but it binds people together. For me, that's the most valuable asset of Ghanaian culture.

How did living in London as a teenager affect your creative approach? — Living in Southwest London had a huge impact on me. There were just so many amazing and exciting subcultures in every corner—the skinheads, the punks, the goths. The music scene was fresh, things weren't mass-produced yet, hip-hop was just coming out and the culture was rather radical and anti-establishment. It was a great time in my life, and it sits really well with me. It sowed the seeds and nurtured the belief that I could do anything I wanted, as long as I did it the right way. Comparatively, Bergen is really quiet, subdued and slow. But as I moved here to raise a family, it was also the perfect place to be in that moment. It's shaped the way I think and do things more than anything or anywhere else.

What's the design community like in Bergen? — The beauty of Bergen is that it's a very small place. It rains often, but the weather helps you bond with the rest of the community as you spend a lot of time indoors, creating things and collaborating. We're all trying to do what we can—individually and together—to enhance the cultural atmosphere of the city.

How has living in these different places influenced your approach to the world? — I've learned to think of people as individuals and not as of different nationalities. It simplifies everything. There are good people everywhere!

Do you feel more comfortable working alone or as part of a team? — In the past, I only liked to work solo—I just couldn't see myself working with anyone else. The design process has nothing to do with democracy: As a designer, you need to dictate how things should be, and hopefully people will get it. But when Alexander Helle and I started Norwegian Rain, the synergy was right. We have a mantra: If I can't convince Alexander about an idea, then it's not a very good idea.

Are you a methodical worker or more impulsive? — I'm definitely a fly-by-the-seat-of-my-pants type. I get inspired when I least expect it, and while working methodically can help to spread out the workload,

Above: T-Michael likes taking visitors from abroad to Mount Fløyen. "It's a great place to recharge your batteries and the view is a bonus," he says. "Getting out of the city is cleansing. The absence of distractions stimulates and reboots your perceptions, and the quietness amplifies everything."

Left: T-Michael wears a Tetteh jacket from his eponymous label and a Raincho jacket by Norwegian Rain. Above: Lysverket, where T-Michael has a personalized drink, is one of his favorite watering holes in Bergen. He has also created uniforms for Lysverket's staff. "I like to sit at the bar, usually alone, and nurse a negroni or whiskey just to allow my thoughts to wander," he says.

Above: Suits designed by T-Michael in Bergen and woven in Sabadell near Barcelona, Spain. To him, the connection between the clothing he creates and the furniture in his home lies in the messages they communicate. "They are functional pieces camouflaged as objects of desire," he says. "They enhance our surroundings either together or separately."

it doesn't really aid my creative process. Sometimes an idea hits me and I have to turn on real quick! I don't fight it—I take it. When I feel really worked up because of a little idea, that's a nice feeling to have.

How do you challenge yourself? — I'm never really content with what I produce. I make notes of thoughts that come up when I'm working on a collection so I can return to them and pursue those ideas as my next projects—it's the only way forward. I feel like I'm constantly challenging myself and don't always need an outside impetus to motivate me, because it's all happening internally. That's what makes it fun.

Please describe your neighborhood. — I live about 60 meters from my store, so I basically just roll out of bed and am at work. My street's pretty hidden and not a lot of people know about it, but it's there for those who know, and that's what I like about it. We don't get hordes of people walking into the store just to avoid the rain—instead we get people that actually want to come in. I've been living on the street for about 18 years now, so it feels like it's my street in a way. It just feels right.

Is your home furnished in a similar aesthetic to your designs? — My home is very much like the way I think. I live in a pretty small flat near the center of town, and I've decorated it with lots of vintage pieces and some items made by friends. Most of the artwork has been bought from people that I know. It only takes about five or 10 minutes to clean it up—it's a pretty portable flat, which is just what I think a flat should be.

Please tell us a bit about your children and what they bring to your life. — My kids are super cool. I bet other parents say that too, but I'm not kidding—mine are *super* cool. They're different in their own ways but they've got the best parts of my ex-wife and me. They really complete me. My daughter is 25 and she's finishing up her master's degree in film studies, and my son is 19 and he starts business school next year. They

keep me well-balanced. I'm a proud papa! My son comes to live with me every other week. It's a wonderful arrangement for us, and parenting at home really helps me take my mind off work. I cook dinner every day of the week when my son's here and my daughter also joins us from time to time. It's very therapeutic.

Do you have any morning routines or favorite coffee shops? — The thing is that I don't drink coffee! I'm one of those people that heads into a coffee shop and thinks, "Oh, this smells so nice," and then says, "One hot chocolate, please!" I drink tea if I'm away from home and people offer me a drink, but I definitely drink more hot chocolate than tea. Bergen is so small that I tend to wind up at the same places every time: I'll go to a coffee shop and end up talking to people I know, or I'll go to the bar and sit down and 10 minutes later my friends will come over. That's what's nice about it—it's almost effortless in a way, and you don't have to plan things too much. My work and my personal life converge, and most of the people I hang around are probably related to my industry in one way or another.

How do you recharge given your hectic lifestyle? — Even though there's a lot of work to be done, it never feels like work. So there's no need to press pause, per se, but it's always nice when I'm not traveling to just sit on the sofa and take a breath—to be *there* for an evening without really thinking gives me the opportunity to let my mind wander. I feel like I've got the right balance in my life at the moment. It feels really good. I like a good whiskey, a good cigar and good food.

What is the driving force that keeps you going when the going gets tough? — Design isn't an easy business—everything that can go wrong in the fashion business usually does. But at the end of the day, I truly love what I do. Just picking up a piece of fabric and thinking, "What can I do with this?" keeps me going every single time. It's an ongoing conversation, and I'm so glad it is.

Left: T-Michael's signature glasses are the product of a collaboration with Dutch designer Ralph Vaessen. "They were handcrafted in Germany and accent my look," he says. The jewelry that he wears every day includes a chunky bracelet by Yvonne Koné, a bracelet by The Caliber Collection fashioned out of reworked illegal firearms and silver rings by Ziva Jelnikar and Henson.

ISSUE TWENTY-ONE CREDITS

SPECIAL THANKS
*Thanks to Katrin Coetzer for
the Starters and Home illustrations*

ON THE COVER
Photograph Pelle Crépin
Styling Carolyne Rapp
Styling Assistant Billy Lobos
Hair and Makeup Dirk Neuhofer
Model Monique at Nevs Model Agency
Casting Sarah Bunter

HOME BLINDNESS
Photograph Frederik Vercruysse
Prop Stylist Laura Praet
Location Graanmarkt 13 in
Antwerp, Belgium

Product
Vase by Nymphenburg

ON PRIVACY
Photograph Frederik Vercruysse
Location The Apartment at Graanmarkt 13
in Antwerp, Belgium
Architecture Vincent Van Duysen

ARCHITECTURE OF HOME
Illustrations Katrin Coetzer

CULT ROOMS: MON ONCLE
Photography Kristofer Johnsson
Special thanks to Elisa Romani at
Les Films de Mon Oncle

SUPER-EGG
Photograph Anders Schønnemann
Set Design Sofie Brünner

Products
Super-egg by Piet Hein,
glass vase by Holmegaard, large vase by
Würtz Ceramics, small vase and sphere
by Anders Arhøj, jug by Anette Friis
Brahe and bonbonnieres by Ditte Fischer,
Broste and Kristina Dam

AMY SALL
Photograph Zoltan Tombor
Special thanks to Sarah Lalenya Kazalski and
Brooke McClelland at See Management

Clothing
Top and skirt by Azede Jean-Pierre, vintage
shoes by Liz Claiborne
and jewelry by Nandi Naya

PETER JENSEN
Photograph Marsý Hild Þórsdóttir
Styling Lilja Hrönn Helgadóttir
Grooming Florence Teerlinck using
Bumble and Bumble and Estée Lauder
Special thanks to Carly Bannerman
and Andy Butcher at Village

Clothing
Page 43: Sweater by Acne Studios,
shirt by Peter Jensen

HIKARI YOKOYAMA
Photographs Marsý Hild Þórsdóttir
Styling Lilja Hrönn Helgadóttir
Hair and Makeup Carly Lim using NARS

Clothing
Page 45: Blazer by Rejina Pyo, bangle by
Maria Black, double ring by URiBE and
Hikari's own silver rings
Page 46: Top by Freya Dalsjø

NEW MINIMALIST: JOSEPH
DIRAND
Retouching Wetouch Imagework
Special thanks to Sofia Di Leva at
DESSELLE & PARTNERS

Clothing
Pages 50 and 60: Top by Ami Paris, trousers
by Acne Studios and shoes by Nike
Page 53: Top by Berluti
Page 59: Top by Berluti, trousers by
Saint Laurent and shoes by Nike
Page 62: Sweater by Ami Paris, T-shirt by
Balmain, trousers by Saint Laurent and
shoes by Nike

OBJECT MATTERS

Styling Assistant Emma Nyboe
Hair and Makeup Marie Thomsen
Special thanks to Alice Mallon

Clothing
Page 65: Jacket and trousers by Soulland
Page 66: Jumpsuit by Henrik Vibskov
Page 68: Blazer by Givenchy, trousers
by Céline and her own jewelry
Page 70: Top by Wood Wood, jacket
by Mark Kenly Domino Tan and trousers
by Won Hundred
Page 71: Top by Filippa K and trousers
by Haider Ackermann
Page 72: Top by Henrik Vibskov and his
own jewelry
Page 74: T-shirt and jacket by Han
Kjøbenhavn and trousers by Won Hundred
Page 75: Jacket by Norse Projects and his
own jewelry
Page 76: Top by Malene Birger and jacket
by Fonnesbech
Page 77: Jacket by Fonnesbech, trousers
by Wood Wood and shoes by Yvonne Koné

REMEMBERED LIGHT

Special thanks to Putri Tan at Gagosian
Gallery in New York

MODERN MOVEMENT

Styling Assistant Billy Lobos
Hair and Makeup Dirk Neuhofer
Model Monique at Nevs Model Agency
Special thanks to Samuel Åberg at Moon
Management, Emmanuel de Bayser,
Steven Haynes, Martina Radonjic and
The Corner Berlin

Clothing and Interiors
Page 85: Dress by Lanvin
Page 87: Trousers by COS, shoes by Robert
Clergerie, cabinet by Charlotte Perriand,
ceramics by Georges Jouve and bowl by
Alexandre Noll
Page 88: Red chair by Pierre Jeanneret,
brown chair and table by Jean Prouvé, lamp
by Serge Mouille, ceramics by Georges

Jouve, bowl by Alexandre Noll and artwork
by Jean Arp
Page 90: Top by J.W.Anderson, skirt by
Mafalda von Hessen, shoes by Gucci, chair
by Jean Royère, stool by Charlotte Perriand
and table by Paul Frankl
Page 91: Bag by Saint Laurent, notebook by
Moleskine, pen by HAY, bowl by Suzanne
Ramié and table and chair by Jean Prouvé
Page 92: Table by Pierre Jeanneret and
ceramics by Pol Chambost and Georges
Jouve
Page 93: Dress by Peter Jensen, shoes by
Céline and couch by Jean Royère
Page 94: Dress by Peter Jensen, couch
by Jean Royère, table, stools and shelf
by Charlotte Perriand and ceramics by
Georges Jouve
Page 96: Top by Rick Owens, trousers by
COS and couch by Jean Royère
Page 97: Bag by Loewe, chair by Pierre
Jeanneret, table by Jean Prouvé, lamp by
Gino Sarfatti, blue and yellow ceramics by
Suzanne Ramié, other ceramics by Georges
Jouve and artwork by Corita Kent

THROUGH A GLASS DARKLY

*All insects kindly borrowed from University
of Copenhagen, Zoological Museum*

Products
Page 104: Box by Michaël Verheyden,
staircase model by Studio Oliver Gustav
Page 106: Lamp by Studio Toogood
Page 107: Bowl by PlueerSmitt for Karakter
Page 108: Candleholder by Patricia Urquiola
for Georg Jensen
Page 110: Marble circles by Kristina Dam
Page 111: Sculpture by Asger Kristensen

VARIATIONS ON SOLITUDE:
GLENN GOULD

*Architectural Historian and Heritage
Consultant* Hagit Hadaya
Special thanks to Kevin Bazzana, Brian
Levine, Faye Perkins, Angus Carroll,
The Glenn Gould Foundation
and The Glenn Gould Estate

TABLE SETTINGS

Horwitz, Jamie, and Paulette Singley, eds.,
Eating Architecture, excerpt from "Table
Settings" by Alex T. Anderson, © 2004
Massachusetts Institute of Technology,
by permission of The MIT Press

LOVER'S DISCOURSE:
VILLA SANTO SOSPIR

Special thanks to Anna Ploman at Link
Deco

IN PRAISE OF SHADOWS

Casting Sarah Bunter
Special thanks to Kevin Keim, Director of
the Charles Moore Foundation
Styling Assistant Maria Rocha
Groomer Sven Bayerbach
Model Mateo at Select Model Management

Clothing
Page 152: Turtleneck and blazer by Issey
Miyake
Page 154: Turtleneck by Damir Doma,
cardigan by CMMN SWDN and trousers
by Margaret Howell
Page 155: Top by Mathew Miller, cardigan
by CMMN SWDN and jacket by Marni
Page 156: Sweater by Marni and blazer
by Joseph
Page 157: Shirt by Lemaire, sweater by
A.P.C., blazer by Hermès, trousers by Marni
and shoes by Grenson
Page 158: Top and neck piece by Lacoste,
jacket by Nanamica, trousers by Paul Smith
and shoes by Grenson
Page 160: Shirt by Dior Homme, sweater by
Joseph and ring by Tom Wood
Page 161: Shirt by Hermès, sweater and
trousers by Margaret Howell and blazer by
Calvin Klein

A.P.C. *apc.fr*	**DITTE FISCHER** *dittefischer.dk*	**JOSEPH** *joseph-fashion.com*	**PIET HEIN** *piethein.com*
ACNE STUDIOS *acnestudios.com*	**FILIPPA K** *filippa-k.com*	**KARAKTER** *karakter-copenhagen.com*	**POL CHAMBOST** *polchambost.fr*
AMI PARIS *amiparis.fr*	**FONNESBECH** *fonnesbech-cph.com*	**KRISTINA DAM** *kristinadam.dk*	**REJINA PYO** *rejinapyo.com*
ANDERS ARHØJ *arhoj.com*	**FREYA DALSJØ** *freyadalsjo.com*	**LANVIN** *lanvin.com*	**RICK OWENS** *rickowens.eu*
FRU BRAHE *frubrahe.dk*	**GEORG JENSEN** *georgjensen.com*	**LEMAIRE** *lemaire.fr*	**ROBERT CLERGERIE** *robertclergerie.com*
ASGER KRISTENSEN *havlitstentoj.dk*	**GIVENCHY** *givenchy.com*	**MAFALDA VON HESSEN** *mafaldavonhessen.com*	**SAINT LAURENT** *ysl.com*
AZEDE JEAN-PIERRE *azedejean-pierre.com*	**GRENSON** *grenson.com*	**MALENE BIRGER** *bymalenebirger.com*	**SERGE MOUILLE** *sergemouille.com*
BALMAIN *balmain.com*	**HAIDER ACKERMANN** *haiderackermann.be*	**MARGARET HOWELL** *margarethowell.co.uk*	**SOULLAND** *soulland.com*
BROSTE *brostecopenhagen.com*	**HAN KJØBENHAVN** *hankjobenhavn.com*	**MARIA BLACK** *maria-black.com*	**STUDIO OLIVER GUSTAV** *shop.olivergustav.com*
CALVIN KLEIN *calvinklein.com*	**HAY** *hay.dk*	**MARK KENLY DOMINO TAN** *markkenlydominotan.com*	**STUDIO TOOGOOD** *t-o-o-g-o-o-d.com*
CÉLINE *celine.com*	**HENRIK VIBSKOV** *henrikvibskov.com*	**MARNI** *marni.com*	**TOM WOOD** *tomwoodproject.com*
CMMN SWDN *cmmn-swdn.com*	**HERMÈS** *hermes.com*	**MATTHEW MILLER** *matthewmillermenswear.com*	**WON HUNDRED** *wonhundred.com*
COS *cosstores.com*	**HOLMEGAARD** *holmegaard.com*	**MICHAËL VERHEYDEN** *michaelverheyden.com*	**WOOD WOOD** *woodwood.dk*
DAMIR DOMA *damirdoma.com*	**ISSEY MIYAKE** *isseymiyake.com*	**NANAMICA** *nanamica.com*	**WÜRTZ CERAMICS** *khwurtz.dk*
DIOR HOMME *dior.com*	**J.W.ANDERSON** *j-w-anderson.com*	**NANDI NAYA** *nandinayanyc.com*	**YVONNE KONÉ** *yvonnekone.com*

Tina Frey Designs
tinafreydesigns.com

tf